COMING
HOME

BLONDEL EVANS-REID

A Comprehensive Guide for Returning Residents

COMING HOME

TATE PUBLISHING
AND ENTERPRISES, LLC

Published by Tate Publishing & Enterprises, LLC
127 E. Trade Center Terrace | Mustang, Oklahoma 73064 USA
1.888.361.9473 | www.tatepublishing.com

Tate Publishing is committed to excellence in the publishing industry. The company reflects the philosophy established by the founders, based on Psalm 68:11,
"The Lord gave the word and great was the company of those who published it."

Published in the United States of America

ISBN: 978-1-62510-112-9
1. Travel / Caribbean & West Indies
2. Travel / General
13.07.01

DEDICATION

This book is dedicated to my husband who has felt so alone for so many days and nights. We were not able to have dinner together as often or to play dominos, our favourite game. I also would like to dedicate this book to all the immigrants all over the world who are thinking of coming home.

ACKNOWLEDGMENTS

I would like to acknowledge my family and friends for listening to me talk about my experience that makes *Coming Home* a reality. I would like to thank my son, Ovando, and my daughter-in-law, Kanika, for their support and encouragement. I would like to thank my nieces Shirlene, Thalia and Melissa for their continuous support and help. Also to Tate Publishing for taking the chance on an unknown; to the staff for their guidance through this journey to make *Coming Home* a book. Only the power of God could make this happen. After my motor vehicular accident I was going through years of treatment I have never asked God "why me", but my song was "One Day at a Time Sweet Jesus." The question I asked my God was, "What is the purpose I am alive? Give me a reason why I am here". As each day went by and I got stronger, I got involved with helping and giving back, and now I have written this book that I believe will help thousands of people. I will interpret it myself that this is the answer. I also believe, with God's continuous blessing, that this is only the beginning.

To two very special people who worked so hard on editing this book: Mrs. Christobel Ansine and Ms. Joan Ansine.

To my beloved elementary teacher, Mrs. Alison Barclay.

CONTENTS

INTRODUCTION

My name is Blondel Evans-Reid. I was born in the district of Clifton Hill, in the Parish of Hanover, Jamaica, in 1953. I have one son who is married, and he has given me three amazing grandchildren, a grandson and two granddaughters.

My parents, Lambert and Eulalee Evans, now deceased, had sixteen children. My dad was a farmer, and my mother was a stay-at-home mom.

There are ten siblings alive. I have many extended families, and we are a very close family. My family are always together celebrating something even when there is nothing to celebrate, for we love being together.

I migrated to Canada when I was twenty-three years old where most of my brothers and sisters lived. We all make that journey to Jamaica as often as we can, and my husband and I do live between Jamaica and Canada.

PREFACE

The book *Coming Home* is not for readers and returning residents not to come home to Jamaica or any other country they wish to return. I have written this book because I believe it will have a positive effect on the lives of all the people who are thinking of coming home to their place of birth. This is an information book about sharing my experience so that returning residents will not make the mistakes that so many of us have made—the mistake of being caught off guard because we did not know. It is for everyone who is thinking about coming home to have the best information they possibly can.

I hope you will read this book and use the information to help make the right decisions. I have tried my best to provide the readers with the most accurate information. I only hope and pray that the lessons I have learned can make a difference in coming home. I am also writing this book for the returning residents who are home to use this book to make a difference and enjoy coming home.

PROLOGUE

How many of us immigrants have constantly told our children and our family that our country of citizen is not our home? We are going home even though we live in that country for over thirty years. Some of us fifty years or more. So many of us have never accepted that our home is where we spent most of our lives, so we told ourselves that we are going home.

We are now retired and now caught between a rock and a hard place because all we think about is going home. Some of us has bought that piece of property a long time ago gradually paying as we get the pay cheques.

I was never that person who wanted to leave Jamaica, but because of circumstances, I migrated. I was twenty-three years of age when I migrated from Jamaica. I lived thirty-five years overseas. Most of my families migrated also. Like most Jamaicans living overseas, we never think of ourselves as a foreigner; we were always a Jamaican. Our culture was very vibrant within us.

We never let go of who we are; we were always a proud Jamaican. Our rich Jamaican culture is very popular within our communities overseas and also our food and our music. Of all the Caribbean islands, Jamaica is probably the most well known. Independence Day is a very important day within the Jamaican community.

It is celebrated all around the world where there is a Jamaican community. This is the day that Jamaica received their independence from Britain. It is a day that is well respected in our adopted countries.

Most big cities overseas join with us to celebrate our independence.

This event usually takes place in the centre of the towns where our flags are proudly displayed, and we are joined by the mayors and other dignitaries of the cities in which we as Jamaicans live.

Jamaica has reached a milestone. We celebrated our fifty years of independence last August 6, 2012. Jamaicans around the globe celebrated this special independence.

Most cities have what is called Jamaica Day, that is when we show off our best—our music and our food including some of our most famous dishes like our curry goat, our jerk chicken and pork, fry dumpling, and rice and peas.

Our food is part of our daily menu at home. The ackee and salt fish is still the Sunday morning breakfast of choice in most Jamaican's homes.

Jamaicans are very proud of their flag, color, and anthem. Many of us still have the plaid clothes we use to have as part of our culture in Jamaica.

Our food is very popular amongst our coworkers; they usually want us to bring Jamaican food for potluck lunch. Our food is well known around the world because of our people sell the best of Jamaica wherever we are in the world.

The bread fruit and ackee plaque, the lady with the basket of fruits on her head, the donkey loaded with the hampers of fruits on our walls in our houses—the Jamaicans overseas all have a little piece of Jamaican inside us not just on our kitchen walls.

The churches will have Jamaican night, the plays from Jamaica, and the gospel singers; all these artists are a success. These functions are always sold out when they are coming overseas to put on a concert. The bumper sticker of Jamaica on our vehicles are always displaying that we are proud Jamaicans no matter what.

Jamaicans overseas are very proud to be Jamaicans. Politics is very strong amongst Jamaicans overseas; we are still The People's National Party and the Jamaica Labour Party. The political conversation is still very strong amongst Jamaicans when we get together. Jamaicans are very much in touch with the everyday function of our country. The Jamaican stores are having a hard time competing with the large chains of grocery stores with our Jamaican produce. Most of the major stores are selling everything Jamaican. The name Jamaica is such a brand. Sometimes we wonder if the produce really comes from Jamaica.

The name Jamaica is such a big seller. These stores can buy in a larger amount than the smaller stores. Therefore, the prices are much more reasonable. Since returning to Jamaica, I can't help thinking if the Jamaicans overseas hold on to their culture more than Jamaicans here at home. When I look around, I am in awe to see how the fast-food stores are doing so well.

The children here don't seem to want their Jamaican food; they prefer the fast food. I was watching a Jamaican school challenge quiz program one evening and the question was asked about the johnnycake, and this child who was about twelve years old did not know what it was.

The other thing I noticed after church on a Sunday afternoon in Montego Bay was that the families and friends are all dressed up from church and having the fast food.

I can't help wondering if Jamaican families are still having the Sunday dinners we had when we were children growing up in Jamaica.

We have so much to be proud of. Until you travel to other countries, then you will realize what we have as Jamaicans. We have a great country. Our culture is to die for; we have so much to celebrate and to be proud of.

My son was ten years old when he migrated from Jamaica. I would send my son home to Jamaica every summer so he could still feel what it is like to maintain this great culture. He is now an adult with three children born in the USA.

Their mother is an American but treasure the gift that these children have both cultures. She enjoys and embraces the culture as much as the children do, and she enjoy everything about Jamaica. The children have been coming back and forth to Jamaica from the time the first child was seven months old.

The culture is alive with my family; my grandchildren will give me a list of what I should prepare for them to eat when they are coming to Jamaica. When they come outside at the airport, they are ready to get into the car to go to grandma and grandpa's house. It is all about the red pea soup with the dumplings and the yellow yam and the Jamaica hard dough bread, and they love to spread on the butter.

Domino playing is a great past time for Jamaicans. My grandson, at six years old, is a good domino player; he can play with fourteen dominoes, so he is learning the game very well. He knows every piece of dominos. He was matching dominos from the age of three. He just loves to play with the dominos because his father taught him. My three-year-old granddaughter is learning to play the game and loves to play.

This is something the family plays together in the winter when they can't kick and throw the ball around. When my grandchildren are in Jamaica, I have to have a plastic bag of peeled sugarcane for them to take to the beach. They look forward to that, and they surely enjoy every bite.

At the time of writing this book, my grandchildren are the ages of four and seven. The oldest is now twenty. My grandchildren love to go to the country where their dad grew up; they love to go to the river, run after the chickens, and go to the bush to see the goats.

I was always in love with Jamaica and returned as often as I could only to see the beauty and the best of Jamaica—the sunshine, the ocean, the food, and all the positive things.

My husband is also in love with this beautiful island, and we surely enjoyed this island to the fullest. We knew one thing for sure, that we would be coming home.

When my husband asked me if I would like to move back home, I said yes. It would not be a problem because the flight was only three to four hours to Jamaica.

Jamaica is the beautiful country that we had left behind, and we were so determined to come back even when our friends begged us not to return; nothing could stop us.

They told us about what they heard and read in the newspaper and the Internet about crimes in Jamaica.

We would not accept what they were saying to us; we were so determined to come home. We told ourselves that nothing would happen to us because we were not in gangs, no family members are involved in that kind of lifestyle, and we were minding our own business.

I feel that Jamaica is one of the very few countries that does not welcome their returning residents. The thing is, from the time we left Jamaica, I would say a good percentage of Jamaicans return at least once every three years or more, while some visit every year.

We have never stopped looking after our loved ones. Who do you think sends the remittance back to Jamaica? The very same returning residents. We have been sending home more remittances than any other country in the world. We have never turned our backs on our relatives we left behind nor have we ever turned our backs on Jamaica.

The problem is why then do we feel so resentful or most of us feel so resented when we come home? We have been so faithful to our country of birth, so why then do we feel that we are the prodigal children who left home and have never returned? We are called all kinds of names when we return home.

Why are we so hated? We are not asking for anything more than the other residents are entitled to. The basic, the rest, we can provide for ourselves.

We lived overseas for many years; we have our families also, but we never forgot our extended families. It did not matter how difficult it was, we always thought of our loved ones home. We try our best constantly to provide for them because we know that no matter how times are hard for us overseas, we believe it is harder for our families in Jamaica.

If Jamaicans would start thinking differently about the returning residents and what we have brought back to Jamaica, I believe that we would not stick out like a sore thumb, and we would feel better about coming home. The other thing is, just imagine how many more would come home. We never stopped loving Jamaica.

The belief that most Jamaicans here have is that when we live overseas, everything come to us very easily. How wrong is the song that they sing. Most Jamaicans have struggled to reach somewhere. Some of us Jamaicans, when we migrated from Jamaica, left children and families who were depending on us to send back the remittance to support them.

At the same time we have to pay to live somewhere; we have to have clothes, different kind of clothes for the weather; and we also have to eat.

Many of us had to have two and three jobs to make ends meet. Some of us even when we were working in the factory tried to go back to school in order to upgrade ourselves.

The journey for some of us is certainly not a bed of roses. Most Jamaicans have that belief, but if they only know the pain and suffering and sacrifice it takes to make it. The breaking news is that not every one made it overseas; some families in Jamaica have never heard from them. They don't know if they are alive or dead.

This is the typical life of so many families living overseas: while the fathers are at work at night, the mothers are at home with the kids. Dad comes home in the morning trying to sleep while he is still the babysitter. He tries to sleep while the children are sleeping while the mother is at work.

The returning residents who are coming home to Jamaica are the Jamaicans who went overseas during the hard times. These are the Jamaicans who paved the rough road. Even if you were a teacher in Jamaica, you could not be a teacher overseas because your education was not acceptable coming from Jamaica. We all had to start from way down the bottom.

These are the Jamaicans who have to do the menial jobs to get somewhere. These are the Jamaicans who fought for fairness, they fought for respect, and they fought for equality. These are the families who sacrificed to make sure that their families in Jamaica had something. These are the Jamaicans who took one relative at a time overseas; they are the ones who have gone beyond and above the call of duty.

These are the people who are coming home. Please love and respect them; don't envy them. They are the ones who showed the world that Jamaicans are good hardworking people. I wish we could hear all their stories. Hearing them talk about their journey, you would cry with them. I have experienced some of those journeys myself, and I have also heard some of their stories.

For the Jamaicans today who are migrating overseas, the way is now paved; the education from Jamaica is now recognized all over the world. You no longer have to start from the bottom. The world is not asking for experience anymore when you enter into their countries.

These countries accept you for the profession that you have, the education you have, and the professionals that you are. You are accepted for the experience that you have. You are no longer starting at the menial job anymore. If you are a nurse in Jamaica, you are a nurse when you step off the plane to start a new life. The only procedure is to sit the exam to have your license.

If you are a mechanical engineer in Jamaica, you are a mechanical engineer when you step off the plane. If you have your master's degree from a university in Jamaica, nothing will change when you migrate; you just have to show the papers.

Your qualifications from Jamaica will guarantee you a job the world over. Jamaicans who are migrating now have a very easy road. The returning resident have paved the road; it is no longer a rough road. They have changed the way Jamaicans are looked at in regard to education.

Where is the best place for Jamaicans to retire and live and have the pension coming to? The Jamaica government and the people of Jamaica should start thinking if it is in Florida or to our home, Jamaica.

Returning residents have played a major role in the businesses in Jamaica:

Here are a few examples.

a.   The construction industry:

b. Returning residents are constantly keeping this industry going. We have built many new houses, or have built houses for our parents.

c. The hardware stores in Jamaica are major business for the Jamaican economy and more people get jobs. The goods in these stores are improved every day because of the demands of the returning residents who are spending great sums of money in these stores.

d. There are more real estate companies than ever.

e. There are more people hired in many areas like housekeepers and gardeners.

f. The banks are thriving from the returning residents because their pensions come to the banks and the foreign currency for the construction industries.

g. The grocery stores are doing very well also. Look at the grocery carts and look at the people who are pushing them.

These are just a few of the areas in which the returning residents have been playing a major part.

CHAPTER 1

This is the beginning of a new chapter in your lives.

Buying the Property

The two most important things to consider before you start the beginning of a new chapter in your lives or before you buy that property or house are the following:

Family Involvement

1. You must sit with your children and the grandchildren and have a conversation about your intention.

2. Then the next question is, would they be interested in the new beginning, and would they like to be part of it?

Talking It Over

This conversation should include things, like will you be spending more time in Jamaica because of the climate and your age? You need to assure them that you will like them to come as often as they can, and you will come back to visit with them also. Let them know that Jamaica is a beautiful country and that they will enjoy visiting. They can all look at it as a summer home and have the best of both worlds.

I know you might be thinking that it is your money, your life, your business and they have their life to live and I am going to live mine.

But there are so many reasons why it is important to think along these lines.

a. It is an investment.

b. They will be the beneficiaries.

c. Property is not an easy sell in Jamaica. It will take years to sell.

d. If they are going to be part of it, then the location is now taken into consideration. The reason could be that they do not want to be away from the beach, the restaurant, or the activity of the town.

e. You can't go and build where the family land is because sometimes it is not in the location that they are going to be part of.

f. Family land can cause problems after death or even when you are alive.

g. The next thing is your lifestyle—what is it going to be?

h. Church. How far do you want to travel for service, and are you going to be involved in the operation of the church? Is the distance a problem for you?

i. What about eating out? Would you like to go out for a meal and how often?

j. Shopping for groceries. How far would you be travelling when you can't drive anymore? What will be the cost of taxi? As for the grocery store, do I need space to even push a cart?

k. If the sea is to be part of your everyday activity, then how far should the distance be?

l. When the children are visiting, are they going to be staying at a hotel to enjoy the vacation and visit with you for a few days?

    The family travel from a far and should not be in hotel. You want them to enjoy the house. You want them to enjoy some good family time. This kind of get-together is not the same in a hotel.

m. How far is the airport from the house or the distance to travel to get home?

n. Remember the driving here in Jamaica is not the easiest thing; it can be brutal. Night driving in Jamaica is not a very good experience.

o. Once you decide on a neighbourhood that you want to settle in, do not rush to make a decision. The next thing I would suggest is that you rent a house for at least three months and look around the neighbourhood. Talk to the people and ask every question that you could think of.

p. Attend the church in the community even if it is not your denomination.

q. Attend the neighbourhood watch meeting; you can get a lot of information.

r. The reason for the three months in the neigh-bourhood is to help you to make a very impor-tant decision and to know what kind of neigh-bourhood it is.

s. The other advice that I can give you is to not build a very large house. The size of the house will make you a target. The belief is that you are a very rich person since you come from abroad, and they should get some of what you have. They think you owe them because you live overseas.

I am writing this note about a beautiful country called Jamaica—the land of my birth. Some believe that only bad things happen in Jamaica, but that is absolutely not so. The intention of this book, though, is not to prepare you to come to Jamaica, but to prepare you for coming home. While writing this book, three of my relatives from overseas returned and bought houses in Jamaica. We have had three family members who have had their weddings in Jamaica within a two year period.

One of my nephews, who was born in England, returned to Jamaica and celebrated his fiftieth birthday. We have a lot to be proud of with this country and Jamaicans are coming home every day to live.

Jamaica has a lot to offer; the weather is good almost all the time. There are a variety of activities in each of the Parishes, from climbing the falls in St. Ann's to the Jazz Festival in Trelawny, where people from all over the world attend every January. This is just to name a couple. We are a proud nation and are proud to be Jamaicans.

We also have some of the most beautiful beaches around the island, so if you choose to be on the beach all day, you will have a great day. The food in Jamaica is to die for. Our famous Jamaican Jerk style cooking will leave your mouth watering.

This book represents my journey and I have included as much information as possible to aid in a smoother transition process for the return home. I also know of many returning residents who are very comfortable and happy coming home, and would not even go back to the country of current citizenship. I think that maybe I am the only person who paid to replace a stolen passport. This book is meant to give you the information—negative or positive—so that you can make the right decision.

Happy reading.

CHAPTER 2

Coming Home

Our dream to come home began when we started looking for land to purchase, and we found a lot to purchase. There was a problem. We love the lot, but the road was in terrible condition. The road is a public road, but it needed a lot of work to be done. We were told that a new road was in the works to be started. So with faith and hoping for a new road, we began the process and purchased the property.

We had the property for about five years when during that time we started to plant fruit trees. The breadfruit trees, mango trees, ackee trees, avocado trees, and all the fruit trees we could think of we planted. All the fruit trees that we have planted we are now reaping them. We constantly have these trees bearing every year.

After a few years we purchased the land, the time came for us to think about building. We made the application for water and electricity, we started the process to have the blueprint drawn up, and we submitted the blueprint to the parish council. While we were waiting for the approval of the blueprints, we started to prepare the property to start the construction; we hired a bulldozer to prepare the property for the house to be built.

Tips for Buying Property

Jamaica is probably one of the easiest places to buy land. There are lots of properties for sale. There are also some very important rules to follow before you sign on the dotted line. The most important thing to remember is that you are handing over your hard-earned cash.

a. The next and probably one of the most important steps is to make sure that the person selling has the title.

b. Make sure the title is clear and it is the title for that parcel of land.

c. If you see the land and that is the piece of land you want to buy, make your next step; hire a lawyer. It is very important that you get a reputable lawyer. If someone is not recommending that lawyer, then call the law society of Jamaica or the parish you will be buying the land.

d. Make sure you get a surveyor to survey the land before you buy.

e. Make sure there is a road to the property.

f. Make sure you have easy access to electricity.

g. Make sure you have easy access to water.

h. You also need good roads to take you to the property. I can't emphasize enough how important it is to have that.

i. The last but very important rule, please do not buy any land over the telephone. Remember, you don't know who you are talking to. Anyone can sell you a property; don't be a sucker.

Buying a House

There are many houses on the market for sale in Jamaica.

There are many different projects:

- The homes that are for sale: They are not all gated communities. You can have single homes that are small, medium, and large. These houses are on open lots; they have gates and fences.

- Housing projects: Some houses are built and are for sale, or you can buy the lot and build your own house.

The other thing to note is that not all of the housing projects here in Jamaica are houses that are built with blocks of steel. Some of the houses are fabricate material, which means they are not as thick as building with blocks.

- Gated communities: Here you can buy according to the project.

My advice in buying into these projects is to make sure you know what you are getting. It is good to talk to the people who are living in the gated communities to find out if they are happy with the project and if the management of the project are living up to what they have promised. Most people will be honest and will tell you what is happening in that project.

I always believe that once you have the information then you can make the right decisions. The important thing if you decided to purchase is to get a reputable lawyer to handle your business.

CHAPTER 3

Building Our Dream Home
The Construction

The land is prepared for the construction to begin, and the blueprint is ready from the parish council.

The process to start the construction of the house has begun. My husband believed he could do the construction by himself. He hired a surveyor to work with him to find the surveyor poles so that the house would not be built on the other property and to line out the house to start the foundation. We found the surveyor's poles all right. The surveyor did not have any other experience to help my husband to lay out the foundation for the house.

My conclusion is that not that my husband could not be the contractor to build this house, but he has been out of this climate for over fifty years. This project started the second of July when the sun is at the hottest time of the year. I was so worried about my husband in the hot sun; he was not used to that kind of heat. By the end of the day, he was tired and stressed, and the only thing that was accomplished was that he found the surveyor's poles.

My husband and I sat under a shade tree and started talking about what happened, and we decided it was time to get a contractor to build the house.

We left the site and went home to the bed-and-breakfast that we were staying. The next day we decided to go back to the land to plan our next move. There was a house building a few blocks before we got to our house. We saw a gentleman standing at the gate. My husband stopped the vehicle, and we went and introduced ourselves. We told him that we are the couple that is building a few blocks up the road from him.

We started talking, and he too was a returning resident. His house was about halfway done. We asked him if we could look around his house, and while we were walking and looking around, we were talking. We asked him if he was pleased with his builder. He told us that he was not at all satisfied with him, but he heard of a very good builder.

We asked if he knew how to get in touch with him, and he made a telephone call. We spoke with him and arranged to meet with him the next day at this house.

The next day about 10:00 a.m., we met with the builder; we talked and opened up the blueprint to see if he could read a blueprint.

When we were satisfied, we drove to our property for him to see and to talk about the contract. After we were finished looking at the site, we asked him if we could see some of his work under construction or work that he has completed. We followed him to the areas where he was building some houses.

We were impressed with his work and decided to have him work for us to build the house. We completed the deal and decided to start the work right away.

The day came and the foundation was been laid out. I was thrilled because the headache was no longer my husband's.

It was a very happy day for us; our dream home has started. We were coming home. We made arrangement to have the blocks, the sand, the cement, and stones delivered.

The journey to build the house was not an easy task. There were a lot of trials and tribulations.

Payroll was every two weeks, and I would keep a book for when the builder called us for the money, he had to tell me what was done for the two weeks. I would keep a record of the work that was done and the money that he received.

My husband and I would come to Jamaica as often as we could to make sure that the work was done. We also asked a few friends to come and check on the progress. The headache started after about a year and a half of building when we came without informing him that we were coming. That made a big change in deciding to take over the project ourselves.

The house was now at the stage where the roof was on and all the walls were up. My husband decided that he was now going to take control of the rest of building the house.

During the ordeal of building a home, you need to be cautious as people have lost their lives through this process. There are a lot of things you have to put up with and walk away from just to be around to finish your house and live in it.

I will not be writing about it all, but I ask that you be very careful. During this process, there are a lot of heartbreaking stories, some you would never even believe you could experience.

Hints For Proper Building Construction

- Returning residents, please be smart when you are building your house.

- Don't forget almost everyone you meet is planning to outsmart you.

- Some of the contractors will take you to court if you stop the project, so protect yourself.

- If you don't know anything about building and reading blueprints, get professional help. It's worth the money you pay for the advice.

- There is a strong belief that when you are from overseas you are rich but you are not smart.

- They think that you must pay more for everything.

- Don't let another house be built from your house.

- Keep a record of everything you paid out and have them sign for the money.

- Make sure there is a date on everything you signed.

- Before you start any work, come to an agreement.

- Have the agreement drafted and signed by both parties.

- Do not let the materials be delivered all at once.

- You should make sure that the suppliers are respectable companies who will work with you and not with the contractors.

- As for the watchman, you need someone to watch him too.

The Fencing

Building of our fence:

We decided on a concrete fence, and we hired a contractor for the labour, and we supplied the material. He came and measured the area and gave us a price for completion of the fence. My husband and the contractor signed on the dotted line for the price and the time it will take to finish the job.

The job started about two days after the contract was signed. The contractor did not ask for a deposit, and the work started on the Monday. The first week ending on a Friday, the contractor asked for money to pay the workers.

My husband gave him the amount of money he asked for. Monday came, he did not show up for work, but he came to work on the Tuesday. He worked again until the Friday.

There is a trend with most construction workers here in Jamaica; they only work until midday on a Friday. But this particular contractor was not coming to work on a Monday, and he was ready to leave by midday Friday.

The problem now is that he is being paid for work that he has not done. The money would finish before the work is completed.

The work, instead of the three weeks, was now four weeks. The next problem we had was that he was not showing up for work at all. Only the men who were working with him was now coming to work.

The contractor was not answering his cell phone, and the wall had to be finished. The only option was to work with the workers to complete the wall.

I have come to a few conclusions about workers in Jamaica.

   a. The workers do not have any idea on how to do an estimate.

   b. Sometimes the estimate is such an outrageous price. You wonder how they could come to that amount.

   c. They are afraid if they give you the correct estimate you will not give them the job.

   d. Sometimes when you look at the estimate and try to help them to figure out what they are trying to do, you can't even do that.

   e. The other conclusion I believe is that the estimate is correct, but they are not spending enough hours on the job.

   f. Be careful of the amount of money that they are asking you for.

Things Not to Put in Your House

These are things from our experience that I have noticed that you should not have in your house.

All these things cause a variety of problems because of the climate; these things will have to be replaced very often:

   • The locks on your doors should not be chrome or gold plated either inside or outside the house.

   • The showerheads should not be chrome.

- The plastic chairs can be very dangerous. They expand because of the heat and can cause an accident.

- Light fixtures must not be chrome, silver, or gold; they rust after a while.

- The kitchen cabinets from overseas, if they are not solid wood, cannot manage the humidity, which—after a while— causes them to crack, and they fall apart.

- The appliances should not be white toaster, white fridge, white toaster oven, white stove, and white microwave. After a while, they turn into light yellow.

- The windows should be vinyl not wood because in a few years you will have to replace them because of the rain and the sun.

- The wood that you used in the house should not be the regular wood. Jamaica has a problem with an insect that eats the untreated wood and after a few months the untreated wood is infested with this insect and you have to remove all the wood. The best wood to use inside the house is treated wood; this kind of wood will not attract insects.

- We all love to have the hardwood floors; it is softer to walk on because we are at an age where the tiles are hard to walk on. I am not saying not to use hardwood floors in your house but please research it very carefully.

- There are lot of problems with the hardwood floor and the heat. After a while, the floors are lifted up, and it feels that you are walking on cushions because it lifted when you walk on it. I have not met anyone who is completely satisfied with that decision.

- I know some people who have used the hardwood floors believe all kinds of different things: Some believe that it was not done properly while some believe that the problem is the quality of the wood. The tradesmen who put down the floors are all different workers, so how could it be that it is the quality of work?

- I am suggesting that if your intention is to use hardwood floor, talk to other people who have used it so you don't make the same mistake.

The Best Things to Have in Your House:

The windows must have mesh otherwise you will be living with the insects inside the house. You have to live with them anyway, so make sure they are not on the inside.

The best windows to put into your house are the sliding windows. These windows do not have levers that are exposed to the salt air. I have used the winding windows and will shortly have to replace all of them because of the levers that are exposed to the sea salt.

What you might be thinking is that I am living close to the sea so it won't matter you don't have to do any of this. Please, this information is the damage I have witnessed everywhere either near or far from the ocean; it does not matter.

The climate in Jamaica is very humid, and you need to open the windows to get some nice breeze blowing in the house.

Appliances should be stainless steel; it seems a very good mix for the climate in Jamaica. I have bought my stainless steel appliances over seven years now and have not seen any rust on any parts of the appliances. That is why I can recommend stainless steel appliances to you. My friends also have not had any problem with their appliances.

The best kinds of fixtures you can buy are brush nickel; it will not rust.

Try and use all treated wood, especially inside the house like mouldings. The wood that you will be using for the ceiling should also be treated; this is a must-have. This wood will cost a little more than the regular wood, but it is the best thing in the long run.

The stove should be gas stove; it will save you money on the electricity, and when you have power failure or a hurricane, you can still have your hot meal.

The bedroom doors should be steel doors; this is also added security, and they have a complete finish. No problem about varnish; you just wipe the door with soap and water.

For the kitchen cabinets, please use solid wood. Jamaica has a variety of solid wood. Like Quogue, Mahoe, and cedar along with all the other woods.

It is very important to have an area at the back of the yard to cook the fish and roast the bread fruit.

We are home, so let us enjoy the outdoors. We have yearned for this feeling when we were overseas. It is a good feeling to do all these things in the backyard. The house won't smell of the cooking of the fish in the house.

The best paint for painting the outside of your house and wall is to use Trowel On.

Trowel On is an expensive paint but just imagine you never have to paint the outside of your house ever again. The color won't fade or change ever, and the maintenance of constant painting will be a thing of the past.

The Trowel On will require a mason to trowel it on to the concrete. Trowel On comes in five-gallon containers. They have many beautiful colors to choose from. The Trowel On will have to be preordered, and you have to order a certain amount to have it order for you.

The only thing that you have to do is to choose the color. The Trowel On will take about three to four weeks to delivery according to the amount.

Hurricanes

Hurricanes in Jamaica

It is almost a surety that we will get hurricanes in Jamaica. The forecast from the radios and televisions in Jamaica will tell you the amount of hurricanes that are predicted each year and Jamaica is one of those countries that is included.

The forecast will give you the months when it is starting. Jamaica is in a preparedness mood from June to November.

This does not mean that we are going to experience all of the hurricanes or that we will be having any at all. This information is very important for you to make preparation.

The first thing to think about when you build your house is the roof you; must have hurricane straps before you put on the roof. This is very important because you can have your roof blown away.

The other items to focus on are your windows and doors; you can have them blown away or have water pouring through the windows and doors like a river.

As for the water that will be running from your house-top, please make sure that the water have somewhere to escape because your house and yard will be flooded.

If in the beginning of building your house you have taken all the proper precautions, then all you have to do when the hurricane season comes around is just have hurricane shutters, a generator, cooking gas, a few flashlights, food, and a battery-operated radio. The other things are a cellular phone to contact your family and vehicle with gas.

Lightning Rod

The Importance of Lightning Rod

I was in for a shock of my life when one day I was home and the lighting was flashing like I have never seen before.

The next thing I noticed was that there was a flash of light that surrounded us. I was so scared and frightened of this light as if it had hit the house. The security alarm went off, which was the first sign that something had happened.

We started to look around to see if there was any damage; we noticed that the television would not come on when we tried to turn it on. The alarm could not be armed.

We then realized that the house was hit by lighting, the security electrical box was damage, the televisions were damaged, the electrical box at the gate was damaged; we could not open the gate by the remote. This damage was very expensive. We had to replace all these items.

When we called the technician to repair the gate, he told us that we were hit by lighting and asked if we did not have lighting rod protector.

I asked him what was that, and he explained that it is a rod that is on the ground and stretches above the roof from one corner of the house to the next.

I told him I had never heard of this before. He said that my contractor should have informed me.

I have noticed after my incident that I am now paying more attention to things like this on the news. I have noticed that lighting is a very serious problem in Jamaica. It can cause very serious problem; lighting strike, we know, can kill people. Lighting can strike, setting buildings on fire.

My experience was not a nice one, and if I only had known, I would have put lighting rod protector on my house. I am telling you these are some of the reasons why I have written this book; it is all from experience. This book is all about information to prepare you so that you do not make these mistakes that we have made. All these mistakes have caused us to do these things twice.

The Kitchen

The Problem of Building Your Kitchen:

The most important tip that I can give you when you are making any form of contract for your kitchen is always make that contract in Jamaican dollars. After reading about my kitchen, you will see why.

I started looking for a kitchen cabinet maker to build my kitchen. I started to talk to people and ask questions. I was not getting any good answers, just disappointment and regrets about their kitchens.

I was now left on my own. I was thinking about all of these conversations and one thing came to my mind was that I know what I want and I can read a blueprint.

My husband and I walked into a display office with the sign that say they do kitchen and bathrooms, roof, and garage doors.

We started a conversation and looked around the room at the materials. We decided to use them to build the kitchen. The contractor came to our house and measured the kitchen. I told them what I wanted and how I wanted it to be. I think he was surprised because

I was not letting him tell me what he is going to do for me but how I want him to build my kitchen.

The next request I wanted from him was a drawing of how I wanted the kitchen to look. I want to know if he understood what we were talking about. We set a time for him to take us to show us some of the work that he has done. We traveled all the way to Manchester to look at the work. We asked him to come back with the drawings.

He came back with the carpenter and the drawings. We made some changes, and I gave him a list of other things what I wanted to go into the cabinets, like how I wanted the cabinet doors and what I wanted to be in the drawers. The next visit would be for him to measure the appliances. I did not want him to build the cabinets and then the appliances could not fit.

The next appointment came we drafted a contract for only the cabinet, and if we are satisfied with the cabinet, he would get the contract for the counter. We decided on the kind of wood for the cabinet and the color of the cabinet.

Next were how many sinks in the counter and the shape of the sinks. The next thing was on the time for the completion and the installing of the cabinet. The contractor told us it would be finished in six weeks. My husband told him that he can take up to three months to finish it, not to rush it, since he wanted good quality work.

We agreed on the prices for the cabinets and the down payment. The balance of the contract will be paid in full upon completion.

The three months came and went, and the kitchen cabinet had not been delivered. We called, and we did not have installation for about six months. We were satisfied with the cabinets. We waited with patience for our cabinets. The deal was completed, and we paid in full for the cabinets.

The next stage now was the counter. We decided on the granite, sink, handles, knob, and design. We decided on the time and price. We had the contract drawn up, signed, and paid the deposit with the balance to be paid in full upon completion. We were to have the kitchen counter completed in three months. Again, we waited six months.

This is the story of the contractor:

When we signed the contract, we did all the transaction in Jamaican dollars.

The problem was that he took a year to complete my kitchen. The kitchen was to completed in six months instead it took the contractor one year to complete.

During that time, the Jamaican dollars devaluated. If the contractor has to buy anything from overseas, he would have to pay a higher price for the dollars.

The contractor thinks that we owe him money. He believes that we should give him more money for the kitchen, but we have a binding contract that shows that we held our end of the bargain.

I believe that if you want to take a year to complete a job that should have taken you six months for completion, I owe you nothing. We have a contract; I kept my end of the bargain. What about my compensation? The inconvenience of me without my kitchen?

I have Christmas dinner with my family who traveled from overseas, and I had to put ply wood on the
counter. It is not my fault if you have lost on that contract because you did not hold your end of the bargain.
I paid you in full.

CHAPTER 4

House Insurance

House Insurance in Jamaica

The coverage of house insurance in Jamaica is another story where a lot of things are involved:

a.   Depends on the location of the house

b.   Depends on if it is on a hill or flat area

c.   How close the house is to the sea and river

d.   Is the area prone for flood

e.   The size of the house

f.   The market value of the house

g.   The kind of roof on the house

Taking all of the above into consideration determines the cost of insuring your house. This can cost anywhere from three thousand dollars to over ten thousand US dollars plus tax per year. This coverage covers earthquake and hurricane.

Insurance for the Contents in the House

There is insurance for the contents in the house including theft:

a.   There is a difference for the electronics

b.   There is a difference for the furniture

c. There is a difference for the jewels

The above items also depend on the market value.

The cost of this coverage can start at four hundred US dollars and up plus tax per year.

At the time of writing this book, the percent for tax on goods in Jamaica is 17.5 percent. It is called the GCT (government consumption tax).

The best advice is before you go to visit or call any of these insurance companies, get the names and check the website and learn as much as you can.

Security

Jamaica is not the Jamaica that you know. Sometimes in the conversation when you are talking about growing up in Jamaica you can't even remember if your parents' home have a lock with a key at the front door.

This is the new Jamaica: the first thing you have to think about before you move into your house is security.

Security comes in different ways:

a. Security installed on the windows and door

b. Security by cameras around the house

c. Security by perimeters

d. Security by burglar bars

e. Security by dogs

f. Security by fencing the wall and having a gate

g. Security by firearms

h. Security the panic buttons

Security is a very important part of your life that you have to give serious consideration about once you build your house and decide to live in Jamaica. You need to have peace of mind, and security does give you that. You might think that you only need security only at night. I would say to you no. Security is needed twenty-four hours per day once you are home.

Security on the Windows and Doors

This kind of security means that all your windows and doors are armed, and any intruder who tries to enter, as long as it is armed, you would be aware because of the sound of the alarm.

Most people do not have monitoring system because they have a licensed firearm.

The only problem with not having a monitoring system is your house is not protected when you are not home. It is fine when you are home because you can prepare yourself to take action. The house is not be monitored when you are out of the country.

Security by Cameras

Security by cameras means that there is a record of the activity around your premises. This does not give you much of a protection except that you can see your property from anywhere that you have access to the Internet. This also will have a record of who enters your property.

This kind of security I would advice you to have dogs and firearm for added protection.

Security by Perimeters

This kind of security protects the yard and the house since it surrounds the property; you can walk around the property while it is armed. The perimeters are installed facing each other to create a zone. The bigger the property, the more perimeters there are.

This security does not allow you to have pets around the yard; it is very sensitive. The alarm can be triggered by a bird once it passes inside the zone.

Once the perimeters are around the yard, you do not need any security on the house. Some people who use the perimeters do not have any burglar bars on the windows and doors either.

The most effective way for the perimeters to work is to have your yard fence then have the perimeters erected around your yard. If any intruder enters your property, they can only enter by climbing your fence.

Before the intruder reaches your house, he will have to cross one of the perimeters. The alarm will notify you and the monitoring station will also be notified. You will prepare yourself that you have an intruder.

I call the security perimeters a watchdog, it barks, which is the sound of the alarms to alert you.

This kind of security is very effective given the fact that you have more time to get yourself prepared. The intruder will have to climb the fence then have to run to the house then prepare to break a window or a door to enter.

With the time it takes him to do all of that, if you have a firearm, he will not make it into your house alive.

If you don't have a firearm, the security company will be there within five to ten minutes. That will give you time to protect yourself with other method. This kind of security will monitor your house even when you are overseas. You don't have to give the company any keys to your house.

The only thing is to notify the monitoring company when you are going out of town and a contact number and when you will be back. This will make the security company fully aware that someone is at your house.

The other thing is that you must notify the company if you have given someone access to your house and the name and the telephone number of that individual. You don't want them to shoot and ask questions after.

Security by Burglar Bars, Dogs, and Fence

Most people put burglar bars on their houses—all the windows, the back doors, and the front porch. The next step is to have the yard fence. There are few different things to use to fence the yard.

a. Some fencing are done with concrete wall

b. Some use wire fence with flowers with a lot of sharp thorns or prickles

c. Some use steel fence

d. Some use wall fence and steel

e. Some have mesh fence

f.   Some fence is done with half wall and sharp thorns or prickles complete the wall.

These fences vary by different height and size; some fences also have a lot of creativity and style and color.

To complete this kind of security, you need a few watchdogs. There is no monitoring cost but lots of caring for the dogs. The other problem: you can't leave the house for any length of time without asking someone to take care of the dogs.

Some people will use the dogs even when they have security on the windows and doors. There are a few people who have dogs with security, and when they are leaving, they put the dogs in a shelter till they return.

The above information is just to give you options. Some things to take into consideration are the following:

- A burglar bars take a lot of upkeep. The best place to put them, the ones for the windows and doors, are inside the house.

- Dogs are a good idea to have as part of your security, but what about if you are only spending some time here and some overseas? The dog becomes another area that you have to make preparations for.

- The security company you will be using for monitoring and to install the security on your property is another consideration. Find out if your neighbour has security and if they are satisfied with the service. Talk to the friends you have and you will get the best result.

- The security company must be reliable. Make sure they are not very far from your house. The time that it takes to get to your property is very important. It can be the difference between life and death. The time from their location to your house should not be more than or about seven minutes.

Firearms

Is it a good thing to own a firearm?

Look at some of the good and bad reasons:

You must have the firearm on you at all times.

Another thing, what if a gunman caught you off guard and you cannot use that firearm?

Are you likely to be killed and the gun is gone?

When you have a firearm, you have to remember that the gunmen are more skilled than you are.

The gunmen have nothing to live for, so killing for them meant absolutely nothing.

What if you only have only one firearm when you leave the house and your wife is home, is there any protection for her?

The other question is carrying a firearm: does it make you any safer?

Having a firearm is a difficult decision. If you are only planning to have a firearm, it is not enough. I believe you need all the above to work with the firearm.

What if you are going away? How is the house going to be protected? This is a major investment, and you have to protect it.

The choice of having a firearm, I believe, is up to you and that decision you will have to make on your own. The main thing that you have to take into consideration is if you can handle the consequence after you press that trigger.

The other thing to know is that for you to get a firearm license in Jamaica, a police report from overseas is required.

The Panic Button

This is a small button that you keep on you at all times; you can put anywhere on your body. This button can send a signal to the security monitoring centre without any noise. The panic button can send a signal even when the system is not armed. This panic button is set up so that when the monitoring centre receives the signal, they know you are in a panic and something is wrong.

Gate Opener and Garage Door Opener

Gate Opener

Gate opener is a very valuable part of your daily protection. Without a gate opener, you are putting yourself at risk.

I am not saying that because you have a gate opener nothing will happen to you. I am just saying that you are more exposed. The reason is that you have to get out of your vehicle to open your gate.

Then drive the vehicle in the garage or the yard and then get out of the vehicle, walk back to the gate to close it, and then locked it with the key. The process is the problem and if you are late coming in.

The difference with the gate opener is that you drive to your gate, press a button and the gate is open, and you drive in and the gate will be closed and lock by the time you park the vehicle.

This is why it is very important to have a respectable company to install the gate control for you. There are a lot of things that can go wrong if the person who is installing it does not know what they are doing. Treat this as if you are buying a very valuable piece of item.

Make sure you get value for this equipment that you are installing. It is an investment and convenience, so find out from your friends about the company that they are using. Would they recommend them to you?

Garage Door

Garage door is also another important investment, so you need the best quality material for the garage door.

The one that we have used is vinyl, and it has stand up very well with the sea spray. We have it now for about six years and have not noticed any rust or crack with this material.

The best thing to do is to investigate and ask questions. Talk to the companies; there are so many all over. Just make sure you get the best quality.

Talk about the warranty and don't be afraid to talk to people you know. All this information will sure help you to make the best decision.

CHAPTER 5

Relationships, Families, Church, and Friends

Relationships

When you make the decision to move home to Jamaica, you have to realize one thing: you are starting over. A few things are going to change. Even the relationships you have invested so much time and effort into are not just friends you have; it is much more than friends. You are like family.

These friendships went through the ups and downs; these are the friendships that have helped to dry the tears. They bring the soup for you when there is sickness. They have been there when the children were born.

There are many good times—the celebrations, Christmases, many birthdays, graduations, marriages, and christenings. The families take vacations together; you are bonded. The next generations of children have grown up as families. These relationships are also longer than you have lived in Jamaica.

Remember, this is not the Jamaica you have left so many years ago. The friends you have here are not the same if they are still here.

Renewing Acquaintances

   a. The first thing to consider is that everyone or almost everyone you know is no longer in Jamaica, and if they are here, more likely they are living in different parishes than where you are building your house.

b.   The other thing is that you have been away from each other for so long that you're now strangers; you have lost contact unless you were in contact and seeing each other during those many years away from Jamaica.

c.   The many trips that you have made to Jamaica and you go back to the district that you are from are because of your parents. Your friends or schoolmates are no longer in that area.

d.   You have nothing in common with each other. Most likely, you can't even have a conversation with each other.

e.   You can't even remember the stories of when you were growing up and in school. You don't remember each other.

f.   The problem is that you have left each other for so long you might be lucky if you have seen each other two times since you have left Jamaica.

The other thing I have noticed is that female returning residents seem to have a harder time adjusting. The husbands seem to adjust much easier. The men can hangout almost anywhere, but the women can't do that. The men can go out and play dominos or go for a drink next door; the women will not do that. The men can easily have a conversation and have a good laugh. We women just can't do that. We are not ready to let someone into our lives.

These Are Some of the Beliefs That We Have

1. The belief we have is that it would be easy to meet returning residents because you can relate much easier because of our journey abroad.

2. The problem is that because you are in Jamaica, no one trusts each other; we are afraid.

3. You believe that only Jamaicans who have less than you will be jealous; we are so wrong.

4. The problem is that certain areas in Jamaica have a name to it that you are living and that can cause some problem. It seems that you have more than the other person.

5. The next problem is the size of your house.

6. A returning resident once made this remark to me, "It is very difficult to meet people who are genuine so when I do, I just hold unto the ones who seems real."

7. I met an American lady who is here because of her husband's job in Jamaica. She is here in Montego Bay, and this is what she told me. "It is so hard to break into a relationship in Montego Bay with other ladies just to have brunch or to sit around and talk." She started her own group.

8. I am speaking only about Montego Bay. I'm not saying that all the other parishes are the same.

Churches

These are some places where dress code is a must; this is one place by the time you enter the front door you are judged. The only difference is that the security guard is not there to stop you from entering.

The other places that have dress code the security guard would tell you that you cannot enter so you would leave. The difference with the church is you enter, but you are feeling so lonely.

The problem is because of the way you are dressed and the clothes you are wearing. It is not that you are baring your skin but because you are wearing a sleeveless. The people in the church have already judged you, so you feel uncomfortable.

You are treated very differently because your attire does not fit the norm of the church. You just don't feel that you fit into that group even though that is the church you are a member of. If you have to take part in a funeral and you are not a member of that church, you are told about the attire to wear in that church.

My husband and I are not of the same religion, so I visited my husband's church sometimes while I visited many of my churches in the area to see which one I would transfer my membership to.

It is very scary to see the difference in the two churches: the ones in Jamaica and the ones overseas. I have a problem with the way the ministers preached of the fire and brimstone of God because I know that the God I worship is a loving God. This is the way I feel when I attended the churches here in Jamaica that I am a member of.

I personally felt very uncomfortable attending services, and these are some of the reasons. The experience varies from church to church.

    a. When you enter the church, you might be lucky if you have someone to seat you. So you seat yourself and the next person comes and sits beside you.

    b. Then there are two people sitting on both sides of you and they will start a conversation while you are in the middle, and the conversation will continue without even saying good morning to you.

    c. This is your first time attending this church and you are walking into church; someone was very polite and said good morning to you. It is a good feeling. I started to feel that this church is a friendly congregation and I am now feeling good to continue my walk into the church. I took a seat it so happens that I am sitting beside the same lady who said hello to me. The service started and she never said another word to me even during the welcome.

    d. The belief that it would be easier to meet people going to the church is wrong; you have to remember that you are a stranger. The cliques are already there; the seats are already marked.

e. You are so lonely. Lucky if you get a hello when you enter, but when it is time for welcome, everyone is willing to say hello and shake your hands.

f. Some of the people who are shaking your hands unfortunately cannot even look you into your eyes; they are shaking your hands but are looking other places.

g. After the service, you can see the friends and the buddies. These are the same people who say hello to you in church but see you in the grocery store or on the street pretend that they don't even know you.

h. You might say then, "Why don't you say hello?" because they might not see you. The answer you get is so cold.

i. I won't name any religions denominations. The other problem that I find also depends on the religion that you were member of overseas also plays a major role. The moment you step into the church, you are judged because of the way you are dressed.

j. If you do not cover your arms or your neck or if you are wearing pants or even wearing makeup, you could not be of that faith.

k. The other thing that I noticed with religions denominations here in Jamaica is that it seems like you are being watched—the clothes you wear whether you are in the church or on the street. The fact that Jamaica has a very hot climate makes no difference to the rules—no flip-flops and no sleeveless inside the church. On the street, no pants and no shorts and no clothes exposing any part of your body.

Remember that the Jamaica you left many years ago is not the same. The changes are drastic; you will be very surprised. The more you are here, the more you see. Then you started to wonder if you have made the right decision in coming home. Coming home to Jamaica required major adjustments. The feeling is that you are starting all over again. The feeling of coming home to Jamaica is like when you first migrated to live overseas. The only difference is that you were younger, full of energy, and ready for the new challenges.

Families

Everything is good or very good when you are overseas with the families you have in Jamaica.

Some of us have so much trust in our families that we send the money to build the house while we are working so hard and sacrificing so much to build this house.

The thing is that these family members believe that because you are overseas you have lots of money.

These family members whom you have trust with all of your life savings when you asked them to build the house for you are not the same. They have changed; they see you as a different person. You are living overseas, you have money, and you can build another house. The land you bought yourself because you would like to make the choice of where you wanted to live if it is not family land.

The next step is that you prepare the blueprint and you submitted it to the parish council, but you never return while it was building.

The journey started, and you are now very excited; you are now building your house because you are now getting pictures of the progress of your house so you work even harder.

The pictures finally show that you are almost there. The dream you believe is now a reality. While working and building the house, you are also shopping for things for the container.

This is the visit to finalize the big move home. You receive the shock of your life when you reach the location to see your dream house. A few of you are very lucky because you see a construction of some sort.

Some of you are not so lucky. The container is at the wharf waiting to be cleared and picked up, but there is no house to bring the container to.

There are a lot of sad stories to be told from returning residents.

This is the family member you trust the money is either spent on building their house or is used for other things.

When you are living here, things are going to change because your circumstances are also changed.

When you are visiting, you always have a lot of goodies; you also ship the barrels as often as you can.

While you are overseas, you were working and you could send the money for them. They love you dearly, but things will change once you come home for good. All the goodies have stop coming because you are now home.

This changes everything in the relationship with your families. They see you a different person; you are not the nice person you were. You are now the mean, awful person and they want nothing to do with you.

Friends from Overseas

You have friends overseas that you spend a lot of time with. Some of these friends have also come home. While you are overseas, you have made plans that you will see each other as often as you can.

The problem you did not foresee is that they live in a different parish than you. They might be living in St. Thomas and you are living in St. James.

Reality sets in after you all settle in; you then realized that it is not so easy to travel back and forth as you think. The driving is not so easy; the distance will take you a day just to reach the destination.

After visiting a few times, you realized that you can't do that driving yourself anymore; you will have to get a driver. The driver can drive you, but the problem is that you tried to but it did not last for very long. After that, you realized that the journey is just too much for you so gradually the time goes you don't even see each other again.

The only thing that keeps that relationship going is the telephone or, if you are lucky, see each other overseas.

I personally have a problem with the roads, even the main roads. The roads that have a lot of twist and turn and are narrow make me very nervous. I am afraid because the other drivers are speeding and are not staying on their side of the road. Jamaica has a high rate of motor vehicular accidents and deaths because of speeding and overtaking. The other problem about driving is the night driving; the drivers still speed and the bright light is still coming at you.

CHAPTER 6

Customer Service and Warranty

Customer service in Jamaica seems that it does not exist. The business does not respect their services and customers. They do not respect the service they offer the customers. Warranty is another problem. I don't know if it is because we do not have the variety of businesses that's why the services are so poor.

My telephones were all out of service one morning; I believe they need batteries, but it was not batteries, there were other things wrong. I drove around town trying to find a store to buy a telephone for the house line. I walked into a store and bought a telephone and was told about the warranty that I can bring it back within seven days for full refund. I was very pleased knowing that if the phone is not to my expectation I can return without any problem.

I went home to open the package and looked at the instruction; I could not read it. The instruction was all in Spanish. I decided I would still plug the phone in and still test it for a few days even though I could not read the instruction. I had no plans to go back to the area for a few days.

I used the phone except that I noticed the volume on the phone was very low. I took the telephone back to the store and told the sales clerk what the problem was. She said she was not aware that the instruction was only in Spanish. She said to me that she could go on the computer and print me the instruction for the telephone in English.

I asked her how the company can bring goods to be sold in Jamaica and it is not written in the official language of the country, which is English. I asked her if there is a bureau of standard for goods to come into the country. If the company can do this with the instructions, I wonder what the quality of the goods that we receive are like.

I told her about the volume of the telephone and that it is very low even when it is on high. She told me she cannot take back the telephone because nothing is wrong with the phone. The salesperson then told me only if the problem was based on the manufacturer's fault could she take back the phone.

I asked her if I could speak to a supervisor; she told me that there is no supervisor available and only she is in the store. It is no longer a conversation but a shouting match with me demanding to speak to a supervisor. I was very surprised that the security guard did not ask me to leave.

It was my luck that day the telephone rang and the person at the other end heard me asking to speak to a supervisor. She handed me the telephone, and I introduce myself and asked for his name.

I told him about the problem and the service. His response to me was that he was sorry about the instruction and his company was not aware that this batch of telephone's instruction was only in Spanish. He told me that he is going to remove the telephones until he put English instruction in all of the packages.

The other problem about the volume on the phone was not enough reason to take back the telephone. The reason is that if his company is to send back that telephone to the manufacturer, his company will have to pay the shipping cost from Jamaica and back.

What he can do for me is that he has some other telephones coming in next week, and he will let me get one of those telephones. I told him to let the salesperson know about this new arrangement. I handed her the telephone and waited until she finished talking. I asked her if she could call me when the new telephones arrived, and she told me yes.

I would be waiting and till this day I never received a telephone call from her. I went into the store with the telephone about ten days after and got the new phone.

The question you might ask yourself is this: Should I call the bureau of standard? Then the next question is, why? I have come to my own conclusion that I would be wasting my time. Here is why I think the way I do. The system is in place for these companies to do the right thing. These telephones were not manufactured in Jamaica. They were imported into Jamaica.

How can these telephones come into the country without being checked? The other thing is that the company that is selling these telephones are not just a single store but a large company.

They have many stores, and in some towns, they have more than one store. There is no policy in place for those goods to be checked to make sure that the consumers are getting value for their money.

The excuse about paying the shipping charges leaves us with the same thing all the time. We, the consumers, in Jamaica are the loser. It does not seem that we have anyone to stand up for us.

Then after you go through the process you then asked yourself about the system because if I, as a single person and not a business, should buy a product from overseas and put into my barrel with the other few items, the amount of duty that I have to pay to clear this item is like buying this product twice. The system is set up so that you cannot bring anything in Jamaica. This conclusion is my own, and if I am wrong, I am sorry, but this is the way I feel.

A Customer Service Agent

This is a job well done.

I have two experiences that I would like to share about a young lady I met. I am going to call her Nicky. The other lady is Chantel at the funeral home when I was preparing for my mother's funeral.

This is a good story about a customer service representative I met. I met quite a few customer service agents during my journey, and they all leave you with something. You think about how pleasant this person is. I have also met quite a few people who you would say that this person left you impressed because they know their job very well. But this young lady, she leaves you breathless.

I have a lot of problem with a company I dealt with in Jamaica, and they did not honour their warranty. It took me about three years of calling, and no one would listen to me. The customer service manager at the time would not do anything to resolve the problem.

I was about ready to get a lawyer when my husband said called one more time and tell the company what our intentions are, and we will not be calling again, but the next contact would be from our lawyer.

That was the day that everything changed. I called and asked to speak to the customer service manager.

I was then transfer to Nicky. She introduced herself. I told her the problems, and she listened and after the conversation told me that she was new to this company and had not seen any report on this work.

Nicky told me that she had all the information, and she gave me a date when a sales manager will visit with me and that the company will honor their warranty.

This customer service manager honored her word. The day came, and the salesman was there with a few other worker. The company has honored all their commitments.

This experience has left me with only one thing: Nicky, all I can say is that you are the right person for the job. You have all what it takes to be a customer service manager. You sure make a difference. Wish you luck.

Chantel was the funeral director at the funeral home where the remains of my mother were, and this is one person I also believe was made for this job. It was a time when your mother was no longer with you, but this lady when she was finished working with me, she made me feel that my mother remains were well taken care of. She is someone whom you could tell her all your concerns and she will make it right. It was a pleasure to work with her; she makes you feel that everything was taken care of.

The Deposit for Goods

The other problem my husband and myself faced is when you walk into a store here in Jamaica and ask the sales personnel to sell you certain items and they tell you it has to be ordered for they do not have the amount you need.

The sales clerk asks you for 65 percent for the down payment and the balance within a few weeks. You now pay the full amount for the goods before you received the goods.

Then the time they told you that it will be ready for pick up sometimes it is months after before you received the goods. Your hands are now tied because you have no choice but to wait until they called you for the goods.

The Telephone Company

I was home one day when my telephone rang. I answered the phone and some telemarketer was on the line promoting some service for the telephone company. I listened to the promotion and then told the person I was not interested at this time and hang up the phone.

When my telephone bill came and I checked it, I notice that these charges were now on my bill. I called the customer service department and explained to the agent. She told me that she will adjust my telephone bill.

The agent told me the amount that I should now pay. I took her name and wrote it down on the bill. My husband went and paid the amount that I was told. I now believe everything is now normal.

I went overseas. My husband was here at home when he called to tell me that he received a telephone call from the company that our bill is passed due to being paid. I gave my husband the instruction and where to find the bill with all the information. He called the telephone company again; we thought everything was now normal.

A few days after, my husband called me to tell me that the telephone is disconnected. The telephone plays a major part in our household because our security depends on it.

We now have no telephone, so we have no security. My husband called them and they told him he has to pay the balance of the telephone and the connection fee. He was also told that it will take about five to six business days to be connected.

The questions that I would like to asked the telephone company are these:

a. Has this account ever been late?

b. Has this account ever carried a balance?

c. Has this account ever been behind with the payment?

I cannot understand why this account was disconnected. Why could this small amount not be carried over to the next month's bill? What happens to customer loyalty? My husband suffered through the pain of not having any security.

The important thing is that this incident could have been avoided. He had to go through sleepless nights and all the other anxiety.

I returned from overseas, and the next day we went to the office with the bill.

I went to the customer service agent, took a seat, explained the matter, and what I got is an "I am sorry." They don't have any idea what happened. The nightmare because of what they have done.

The stress for only about two thousand dollars is such a menial amount of money. Where is the human side of the company? Do they care?

Or it is all about the money, bottom line? My husband could have been killed because of two thousand dollars, and it was not even our fault.

You are not getting back your money either. The only thing that you will hear is your bill will be adjusted on your next bill. Is this the way to gamble with people's life? No. I also know you are running a business but show too that you care. Let us put a human touch on the business.

This was an account in very good standing; we did not deserve this kind of treatment.

The other problems that you have to deal with are the companies who have to custom-order things for the bathrooms or other things that have to be measured. Items like shower doors, cupboards, and cabinets.

They come and measure the area then give you a price and the time it will be delivered. You agree with all the terms of the contract, including the terms of the payment and deposit.

The date of the contract is passed, and you hear nothing from the company. The next thing you do is call someone in the office and ask for certain person. You are told he is not in the office.

After a few phone calls, you decided to drive to the location. You asked to see the person. You are told he will be with you shortly; you waited. He came but with all kind of stories. You asked why he did not call you or return your call and why you have to call him.

You are now passed a month over the due date and no answer. The company now have your money, and you are now stuck.

My husband is now ready to be a nasty person and is now ready to get angry. He now believes that he has waited long enough and is time for his money or the goods.

It was not a nice day, and he did not care about the other customers who were in the store. He was asking for his money back; he waited long enough.

You know there were other customers in the store with the same problem. My husband did not want a cheque either because he did not trust the company by now; he gave the company cash, and he wanted back his cash. He got back his money and walked out.

These are some things that I notice about customer service here in Jamaica. When there is a problem, if you are not angry and start to be nasty, nothing is done. Why does it have to reach to the boiling point before we can have anything done?

I still believe things can be done much easier. We need to start with respecting the rights and dignity of each other. We need to stop the belief that we are better than the other person.

This class business needs to stop, and if we realize that the only thing that separates one from the other is opportunity, we will all make a difference.

Paying My Bills

There are some stores that you can pay your bills hassle free for a minimal fee.

They are always close by to where you live, close to a place where you always shop so you don't have to go out of your way. Parking is hassle free. I always pay my bill at the same location. I never check to see if anything was wrong until I have a problem: my water bill was not paid.

The next month, the bill came, and my husband went to pay the bill. He came back with the bill, put it on the counter, and I was curious to see how much water was used this month. When I opened the bill, I noticed that even though the bill was paid last month it still showed the balance brought forward. I know that I paid this bill before. I looked at last month's bill and it was paid.

I called the accounts department of the water commission and spoke to a customer service agent. She said it shows that my bill was not paid last month.

I told her that yes it was paid. I have the receipt in my hand. She said to me, "Let's see what account it

Coming Home

was paid to." She was absolutely right; it was paid to another account.

I asked my husband to take the receipts back to the clerk at the location where we paid the bill and showed them the problem. He took it back. The customer agent told him the adjustment will be shown on his next month's bill, and we will not have to pay any money for next month's bill unless we used more than the last bill.

The water bill came with the amount to be paid, and no adjustment was made. I decided I will go to the office myself. I gave the clerk all my receipts and bills then I explained the problem. I told her it has been going on for two months now, and I will not be waiting again for the next month for the adjustment to be made. I waited for about thirty minutes for the adjustment to be done, but it was completed.

I was told that I had to pay the service fee. I could not understand how I have to pay that service fee again when I have paid for that service already. The other thing is that I was not the one who paid the bill to another account. The clerk gave me a choice: either it is carried over on my next bill or I pay now.

I know that it is not a large amount of service charge, but what about my rights? I have to pay twice for the same service. I could not waste my time and energy anymore. I paid the money, took my receipt, and left.

The lesson from this incident is that before you walk out, step away from the counter and check your receipt.

81

Painting My House
The Paint Company

I will not be naming the company, but I will talk about my experience buying paint and painting my house. I have painted my house over six years to the time when we decided some areas needed repainting. We also have some new areas to be painted. I went to the hardware store and was introduced to paint that I have not used before or even heard of. I have dealt with the salesperson before, so I took his recommendation and bought the paint.

I painted the new areas and repainted the old areas. The job was completed, and the colors were beautiful except that after about three months I noticed that the areas were peeling, not just the new areas but also the areas that were painted before.

I also noticed that a white color was coming through the other colors of the paint. These areas you could not lean against the wall because you would be covered with white all over your clothes and hand.

The tiles on my front porch that are exposed to the rain started to be covered with this white that is coming from the paint.

I went back to the company that I bought the paint and told them the problem I was having, and I was told that they will get in touch with the paint company and have someone come to look at the house.

I waited for some time for a representative from the paint company to come and see me. Finally, a representative came. He looked around the house, took some samples, and told me that he will be in touch with us shortly.

I waited about six weeks when I received a phone call asking me to pick up a letter from the paint company at the store where I bought the paint.

Lucky me I drove to the store just to get a letter telling me that the delay was from visiting the site and partly from the fact that they had to involve overseas assistance in determine the source of the problem.

The letter stated that the paints meet their usual specifications. However, there is evidence of excessive alkalinity within samples taken from the surface.

This is believed to be caused by chemicals in the concrete, which are released when exposed to moisture leading to discolouration and breakdown of the paint film.

The letter recommended how I am to prepare the concrete to be painted and I am to buy other product from the company to help to prepare the areas before it can be painted. After I spent that money and hired painters to prepare the areas for painting, as a gesture from the company they will give me two gallons of all the color that I have used.

I have paid the painters to paint all these areas but no compensation because the problem is with the concrete and not the paint.

I had a problem with this letter and the response from this paint company. The areas that I have repainted have been painted for over six years with other paint. I have never had a problem with the paint I used before. Therefore, how could it be the concrete?

The other problem I had is not just the concrete that was painted; we also had the eaves around the house painted. I wanted to know what chemical was coming from the wood around the eaves. The areas that are exposed to the sun and rain on my front porch on my tile are covered with this alkalinity.

My question then, is there a default in the wood? The difference is that they did not address the area about the eaves. If there is evidence of excess alkalinity, what about the areas that has been painted for over six years? I have never had a problem with these areas before only that it was time to have the area painted. My question is, how could it be the concrete?

The major building materials in Jamaica are blocks, stone, sand, and cement. Therefore, if it is the concrete that is at fault, then my house will not be the only concrete house that is having problems with the paint that we used.

The other question is why then is this the only paint that I am having a problem with? I have used the paint from the other two major paint companies and have never had a problem after six years.

I started having problem with the paint after three months. I repainted the areas, and by the end of six months, I realized that I have a serious problem. This then is a matter of concern for the consumers.

I will not be walking away with this letter accepting what the company says. If it means that I have to start a revolution with other homeowners who are having problems with this paint company, I will. They either have to change the mixture of the paint or stop selling that paint in Jamaica.

My conclusion about this paint that I bought from Paint Company Color, my name for the company, is that the paint cannot handle the climate in Jamaica. The paint functions well inside the building that is not exposed to the hardship of the outside of the building with the sun and rain. It is just not able to function.

I have used the same concrete outside and inside the house. I have used the same paint inside the house and the same paint outside. The inside paint are just fine; I have no complaint about that. The paint outside are the paint with the excessive alkalinity. At the time of sending my manuscript for editing, I have not solved this problem with this company, but I will still continue.

The conclusion on customer service in Jamaica, from my experience after living overseas for so many years, is that we expect to be treated with respect the same way we have been treated in other countries. We have worked hard for our money, and we should get value for it. I will also said that in Montego Bay there are a few business who are surely going out of their way to give good customer service.

CHAPTER 7

Shopping

Shopping in Jamaica is so much different from shopping overseas. Reasons are that we do not have a wide variety of stores to have the competition we are used to. Therefore we have to make a lot adjustment in regard to shopping.

Grocery shopping: I am not comparing the entire Jamaica because I have not been shopping all over Jamaica. I am only comparing the shops in St. James. One of the problems that face the town of Montego Bay and shopping is about parking.

I must acknowledge that there are some new changes in Montego Bay for the betterment of the town. The town is now moving out to Bogue where there are quite a few stores and plenty of parking also.

The shopping areas are Bogue Shopping Village and Fairview shopping centre and a huge grocery store at Catharine Hall. The parking is great; there are banks, hardware stores, fast food, pharmacy, and many more stores.

The problem with the groceries stores around town are the competition. There are a few grocery stores, but the prices are no different. They are the same or more, so you settle for the one that provided everything the one-stop shopping because you have parking and space to push the cart.

A few banks are also moving into these areas for your banking convenience. There is a new shopping centre in Iron shore called Whitter Village; there are restaurants, clothes, grocery store, and other stores. We also have a variety of other stores and casino across the street.

There is also another area: Parkway mall in Coral Garden. There is a grocery store, hardware store, and other stores. One of the things that I noticed in these stores that are not so good is the familiarity of the cashiers.

When you always have to go into some of the smaller stores all the time to shop, the cashier started to be a nuisance by begging money.

They seem to target the men they believe come from abroad; they beg money to buy credit or money to buy lunch. I know that the owners are not aware of it, but it is happening.

CHAPTER 8

Driving in Jamaica / Insurance / Auto Mechanic

Overseas Driver's License

The foreign driver's license is valid and can be used in Jamaica for three months. This is to allow for you enough time to get your Jamaican driver's license.

Traffic Tickets and Foreign Driver's License:

The latest news up to the time of writing this book is that if the police stop you for speeding or any other traffic offense, you are issued a ticket and on the ticket. There are two options:

Paying Traffic Tickets

1. You have twenty-one days to pay the fine at the collector general's office nearest to you (tax office).

2. If you missed the twenty-one days, the next option is for you to go to court to settle the matter within ten days.

If you missed these two options, the next step is that a warrant is issued for your arrest.

My advice is that if you get a traffic ticket in Jamaica, do the right thing. Pay the fine just like you will pay in any other country and remember that a warrant for your arrest never expires.

The first step to start the process for your Jamaican driver's license is a trip to the tax office in the parish that you live in.

The process for getting your Jamaican driver's license is the following:

a. You have to pay for the examination fee.

b. You need three passport-sized picture.

c. A completed application form for a driver's license.

d. Written test.

e. Driving test.

The application form for a driver's license can be picked up from the tax office at the driver's license department. The three passport-sized photograph signed by a justice of the peace.

The cost for the examination fee is one thousand eight hundred dollars to be paid at the tax office.

You will then be given a document to take to the examination depot where you will have to do a written test and a driving test.

After you have the procedure completed and you have passed the test, you will be given a document to take back to the tax office along with the signed picture and the completed application for your driver's license.

You will have your Jamaican driver's license for four years within a week.

Getting My Drive's License

I had my driver's license before I left Jamaica over thirty seven years ago. I decided that since I am getting all my Jamaican documents I should get my driver's license also.

I was ready to start a battle because I had so many blocks in the way on getting the other documents.

My niece and I were together one day when she saw a friend of hers, and they started talking. One conversation to the next and the conversation of my drivers' license came up and that I was going to start the process to get my license.

I told him that before I left Jamaica I did have a driver's license. He said to me that my information should be on the system. The gentleman told me that I should go to the tax office and give the information.

I went to the tax office in the parish that I was living in thirty-seven years ago. I was in shock the information was there. I was told to bring in three passport-sized photograph to the tax office and pay the amount for the license.

The only thing I had to do was to change my name to my married name. The driver's license was ready within seven days.

The good news is that if you have a driver's license before you leave Jamaica it is very easy to continue where you left off. All you have to do is just go to the tax office with your identification and renew your driver's license.

Motor Vehicle Insurance

Jamaica has a large number of insurance companies for motor vehicles. The best thing to do is to check around to see which is best for you find out what they offer. It is a major task that you will be investing in, so make sure you do it the right way.

A few of the banks also have insurance for vehicles and also health insurance. This is another easy way to make it one-stop shopping. The cost of insuring your vehicle in Jamaica is very costly and time consuming. To insure your motor vehicle required a few things to be done before you can get the vehicle insured.

a. Certificate of the motor vehicle

b. A certification sticker for the vehicle

c. Insurance

Each year to insure your vehicle, the first step is to go to the tax office and pay the money for your vehicle to be certified. Then you go to the examination depot to have your vehicle examined and check to make sure the vehicle is in proper condition.

If the vehicle is not up to standard, the examiner will give you a paper with all the things that need to be fixed. If the vehicle is in proper working condition, then the examiner will give you a document to take back to the tax office with the certification.

The next step is to pay for the sticker that you have to put on the windshield of the vehicle. This sticker is to show that your vehicle is certified for one year.

The next step is for the insurance company to get the insurance for the vehicle. All the documents that you have paid for at the tax office you have to present to the clerk. The insurance company have different kinds of insurance coverage so chose the one best suited for your needs.

The full coverage means that the insurance paid for your vehicle and the other vehicle if you are wrong.

The third-party coverage means that if you are wrong, the insurance company will pay for the other vehicle and you will pay for your own.

The difference between third party and full coverage is that in third party you are not covered for theft or fire; you have to stand all the losses. The full coverage means all and everything.

The most difficult experience here in Jamaica is dealing with the insurance company. Again, I don't know if all the insurance companies are the same and if they all operate the same.

But the experience with the company that we are insured with is not a very good experience.

This is our story of having a minor accident in Jamaica. When this accident happened, we were fully covered. My husband was driving back from St. Elizabeth to Montego Bay through the hill and gully of New Market.

A lady was driving a minivan going in the opposite direction and hit the side of his vehicle. They both stopped and exchanged particulars; he then continued to Montego Bay and stopped at the Coral Garden Police Station to report the accident.

When he went into the police station, he was told that he had to report the accident at the Bethel Town Police Station. The next day, he drove from Montego Bay to Bethel Town Police Station and was told that there was no report of the accident; he had to go to New Market Police Station to report the accident.

My husband drove to New Market Police Station from Bethel Town and was told that there was no report of the accident and was told that he had to go to the Black River Police Station to Report the accident.

He walked out of the police station and drove back to Montego Bay. The next day, he went to the insurance company and reported the incident. The clerk in the claims department told him to go to the main police station in Montego Bay and report the accident.

He went to the police station as he was told to report the accident but was told again by the police officer that he had to go to Black River Police Station. He went back to the insurance company to the clerk in the Claims Department. She told him that there was nothing they could do without the police report.

I have a question in regard to this incident, why can't the police stations take the report from any parish? What is so difficult that the police stations does not communicate with each other?

This process takes a few days back and forth between police and the insurance company and unfortunately my husband had to fix his vehicle himself.

These are the difficulties that one faces in everyday living in Jamaica. The things we take for granted where we were living become so difficult for us.

The most important thing to remember when you have an accident in Jamaica is that it is not like overseas. The first thing you have to do is to telephone the insurance company and the process will begin.

In Jamaica, things are different. You feel like you are on your own. Everything takes a longer time to process. My advice is to have patience and don't give up.

Auto Mechanic

This is another area that can be very painful to deal with: auto mechanic. It is very hard on your nerves. When you have to take your vehicle for repairs and you are told that you need certain parts, the problem is that you buy the parts but the problem still is not fixed. Then you are told that it needed something else and it's still not fixed. This will go on even if you are going to find another mechanic. It is a nightmare to find a good mechanic shop to work on your vehicle.

The motor vehicles parts are very expensive to buy in Jamaica; remember these parts are not manufactured in Jamaica. The consumers have to pay the shipping cost and the added taxes for shipping, and you are charged all these extra money.

CHAPTER 9

The Banking System

The banking system here in Jamaica is not like overseas; you need a full day for banking services. The banks in Jamaica are very busy.

Parking: Only a few banks have parking spaces, especially those in the city. If they do have parking space, it is always very busy. You are lucky if you can find parking. Therefore, you have to find a place to park at another parking area and then walk to the bank, which can be a distance.

Time: When you are planning to go to the bank, you have to prepare to spend the most part of that day or plan to be at the door just when the bank is open.

If you have to meet with a bank supervisor or manager, be warned that you will not be getting their full attention. The bank manager answers every telephone call including the personal cell phones while you are sitting at the desk.

Be prepared that you will be interrupted at least six times by other bank clerks to sign a document or to ask a question.

The lines in the banks are very long; they do have senior citizen chairs, but it is always very busy.

The ATM Machine

The bank machines are a few at a distance. These machines are always busy. The line, when you find one that has money, is very long.

You are stuck in the line waiting because you are not prepared to drive around looking for another machine because you are not going to find parking.

Because these machines are very busy, the machines always run out of money.

You might be lucky to see the security company filling the machines then you can wait up to fifteen minutes or come back another time.

Returning Residents and the Banking System

A lot of returning residents got caught with the banking system here in Jamaica. We were told that we would get a better rate of interest if we were to change our money to Jamaican dollars. The annual rate would be 13 percent for example.

This looks like a good offer, so you go ahead and change the foreign currency to Jamaican and put into the bank with the 13 percent or more.

The plan you have now is that at a certain time you will go and take the interest from your money. The year has come for you to take the interest and to put back the principal. You know that you hear on the radio and the business news about the changes that are been made in the banking system but not knowing that it would affect you. When you go to the bank to do the transaction, you almost have a heart attack because the interest is no longer at 13 percent.

The interest rate is now 3.5 percent if you are lucky. This kind of investment is not a fixed interest and does not guarantee whatever the going rate is that is what you get.

A couple of things happen to you when you change your foreign currency to Jamaican dollars.

The money fluctuates every day in Jamaican dollars.

If in January you change twenty-five thousand US dollars and you get at that time three million Jamaican dollars. In December if you were to change back that money to US dollars, you will not get twenty-five thousand dollars.

You will get far less in US dollars for your twenty-five thousand dollars. This kind of devalue of money will cost you more US dollars to buy back.

So you have lost both ways the devaluation of the currency and the lost in the interest rate.

Transferring Foreign Currency

The Jamaica National Building Society (JNB) is a bank that is very good to work with to send your foreign currency to Jamaica for buying property or building a house.

This bank has locations in most of the cities in Canada, the United Kingdom, and the United States of America. They have a lot to offer; take a look at the web site.

Cost of Living in Jamaica

Jamaica has to import almost everything into the country, and the government has to buy in US dollars. The cost of living, based on the fact that we do not manufacture many goods for ourselves, is extremely high.

The cost of buying food is very expensive, building a house, buying a car—everything comes from foreign countries. My advice is to please have proper financial planning before you make the decision of coming home. The fact that your currency will give you more in the exchange still does not make the cost of living any less.

The cost of buying is still very high and that makes inflation very high. The goods you buy in Jamaica include the shipping and the tax. An example is if you buy a television overseas, you pay the consumer tax on that television. Most stores do not participate in the paperwork to have the tax removed from the item because you are shipping it out of the country. The next step is you have to pay to ship it to Jamaica then you have to pay the duty and pay to clear at custom; it is not worth it to buy that television from overseas. You are better off buying it in Jamaica.

Jamaica General Consumption Tax

This is a general consumption tax (GCT) that is paid on goods and services. It is now calculated at 16.5 percent.

If you have a business, you have to be registered with the government before you can collect this tax from the consumers to file your return to the government.

PHOTOS

CHAPTER 10

Politics in Jamaica

The two party systems both in General and Local Government continue to exist.

While I was writing this book, two elections were held: a general election and a local general election. The general election was announced by the youngest prime minister ever in Jamaica. His name is Andrew Holness. He has been appointed as the prime minister of Jamaica when the then Prime Minister Bruce Golding stepped down.

The election was announced three weeks after Mr. Andrew Holness became the prime minister. The nomination was held on December 12, 2011. At this time, all the candidates registered their intentions that they will be running for their party of choice. This is a very important day for the candidates, and there is a big celebration for each of these candidates. The general election was to be held on December 29, 2011.

Jamaica still has a two-party system: the Jamaican Labour Party, which at the time of writing this book was the party in power and the Prime Minister was Bruce Golding, and the People's National Party where the leader was Mrs. Portia Simpson Miller. Also at the time of writing this book another party was in the process of forming, which is called the National Democratic Movement.

One very important thing to know about these two parties is that they are very color conscious. The

Jamaica Labor Party color is green while the People's National Party is orange. During election time, these colors are very important to the parties, so be conscious about these colors. These colors while wearing could mean something even if you are not part of the political jamboree.

I can say from my observations that the politics that I know when I was growing up in Jamaica has changed for the better. These are the new policies that are implemented for the betterment of election in Jamaica:

1. There is now a political ombudsman of Jamaica.

2. There is a National Integrity Action Limited.

3. There is a Joint Agreement and Declaration on Political Conduct.

4. There is a Code of Political Conduct.

5. There is an agreement and declaration on political conduct.

6. There is Breaches of the Code of Political Conduct.

I have been living between Canada and Jamaica for a while, and I have been observing the changes in the voters. The voters during my parents' days were about buying votes for nothing and the politicians do what they please without accountability.

The only thing that was important those days were to give some basic things and a little bushing of the road and that was enough to have a guarantee vote.

I am not saying it does not exist anymore because a lot is still going on. I am not saying that everything has changed; there is still a lot needed to be changed.

Over the years, I have noticed that the voters are definitely more educated and demanded a lot more from there politicians. If you sit back and watch the news on the television, you will see how they are demanding more—they want better roads, better schools, and they are more involved with the everyday business of the government.

The talk shows on the radios are a very powerful tool to give the voters a place to let the politicians know what they are demanding from them. These outlets are a very good source for their voices to be heard. If you listen to them calling into the programs, they are not accepting no-nonsense politics.

The Jamaican voters are very smart and want their politicians to be accountable. Don't think that politics in Jamaica is like before. It is no longer a free ride; you better perform.

The other thing I have noticed with the general election is that times have certainly changed. I have noticed the difference between the people in the parties. The most interesting thing that I have noticed is the amount of killing during this election.

After this election, the headline for the international newspapers were not be about the amount of killing but who the winning party was.

Election and Christmas

Jamaica does not have a special date for election, and it can be called at any time of the month. I believe it is one of the best election ever to be held in Jamaica in regard to the amount of killings. The voters are definitely not like before. I also noticed that people are more civilized to each other and are friends regardless of the colors each person is wearing. It seems that politics is not coming in between people like before. It seems that they can be a member of a different party and be friends and neighbours.

Election and Christmas sure did not mix in the December 29, 2011, election. What were they thinking? I am not speaking for anyone else but for myself.

The entire process was not good for me. I have also met a lot of frustrated Jamaicans through the process. How could we add more stress to Christmas to such a very busy time? The roads were extra busy, and the towns were already so chaotic.

That is what Christmas time is about now let's add election to that mix and you can imagine what you get. The inconvenience of not been able to do your last-minute shopping. Christmas becomes a stressful time instead of a happy time because everything takes a longer time to complete.

The airports in Jamaica at Christmas are so busy and stressful. Travelling also adds extra stress. The fact that you have been travelling from the early part of the morning to get to the airport, and in the middle of this, you have to deal with the extra congestion.

The plane has landed; you then go through the process, and you finally put your luggage in the vehicle and ready to hit the road. The journey is almost finished. You are so tired and hungry and can't wait to get home.

Put election in the mix and the problem is that you can't even get out from the airport to get on your way because there is a political meeting to be held in the square of the town. A journey that would normally take you two and half hours now will take you about five and half hours. The feeling of anger can't even describe what you are feeling. The problem is you do not even have an alternate route.

The entire Christmas plan changes; you have had enough of the entire confusion and decided to stay off the road. The atmosphere for Christmas now changes; you don't want to even travel to friends and family for the real reason of the holidays. You make a decision to stay home and get out of the madness.

The entire holiday season has changed. My friends who are here visiting just for Christmas week from overseas has lost so many days in visiting friends and family they are not comfortable travelling all over the country as before.

They will call and tell you that they are sorry but because of the atmosphere they will not leave home. They better be safe than sorry.

The air waves should be a happy time just listening to the radios talking about the good news of Christmas and the singing of carols but instead there are all these commercials of politics.

The commercials are so overpowering. The atmosphere of Christmas has already be ruined that the only choice you have is to turn off the radio.

The people are almost in the middle of the road. You can't even see them while you are driving. You are just praying that you don't hit anyone.

The Election

Well, the election come and gone, and I was right with my observance about the voters. This is a day that all Jamaicans should be proud of themselves whether you live in Jamaica or any other parts of the world. Jamaica has had an election day that will go down in history as one of the best day. It is the most amazing election ever held.

The election was held on the twenty-ninth of December 2011. There were only a few minor incidents. Compared to all the other elections that has gone before this one, this is an election to talk about. The results of the boxes were very impressive and how quickly they were counted and announced. It was exciting watching the results. The polling stations were closed at 5:00 p.m., and the winner was predicted and announced by about 8:30 p.m. This election results sitting in my living room watching the result made me feel that I was watching an election result in some foreign country and not in a third-world country. Well done, Jamaica.

The Peoples National Party won a majority government with forty-two seats and the Jamaican Labour Party with twenty-one seats. The Jamaica government had a sixty-three-seats parliament. I was also impressed the day after the election how peaceful the country was while they were celebrating.

The next election, which was the local election, was held on Monday, March 26, 2012. This election is the process of how the mayors and councillors are elected. The majority of the seats were won by the Peoples National Party. This election was also a quite campaign.

CHAPTER 11

Hospitals

Public and Private Hospital and Health Insurance

I must start this chapter by saying that Jamaica has some of the best doctors and nurses in the world. When you consider the circumstances that they have to work under, they don't have a lot of equipment to carry out their jobs. They don't always have the best atmosphere to carry out their duty, but they surely do their jobs. I personally have a great deal of respect for them.

I must also say that Jamaican nurses are highly respected in North America. These professional are highly trained. When I visited these hospitals and saw how sick these patients were and to survive these kinds of sickness with the help of the doctors and nurses, I am very proud to see the quality of work they can provide.

I notice that they do their best for the patients to get them better. I believe that these professionals do care about their patients in Jamaica. I have not been into all but a few hospitals.

Public Hospitals

The public hospitals I had the opportunity to visit in Jamaica have been an eye-opener for me. The word *health care* in Jamaica is free. Let us stop for a second and ask what kind of service is free.

I do not want to get into politics in Jamaica but because my husband has been constantly asked about filling the forms to get free medication it caused me to ask these questions. The question that I asked was: Does Jamaica manufacture medicine?

The answer is no. They have to buy the medicine from overseas in US dollars. The next question is, Where does the Jamaica government get the foreign currency from to buy all these medication?

I have seen my friends who have had a mammogram done but had to purchase the biopsy needle and then take it to the doctor to have the test done.

I have read in the gleaner where women who have to have the biopsy after the mammogram shows that there is a lump in the breast but not able to buy that needle to complete that test.

I am not getting into the politics in Jamaica as I said but I would just like to have these questions answered.

Whenever my husband is to fill a prescription at the drugstore, the pharmacist is always telling him to fill out the form to get free prescription.

She is always putting the forms in the bag with the medication. My husband's response to her is that the government cannot afford to give him prescription.

I mentioned about the medication, which is free for everyone in Jamaica. I want to bring attention to this, how do you stop the drain of this system when it is available for everyone? How can the distribution of the mediation be controlled when it is available to all Jamaicans, even the ones who can afford it?

The other things that I noticed in the hospitals that I have visited are the cleaning. When I am visiting a patient on the ward, I always wonder if there is any pride in the way the work is done. I had a conversation with a very prominent business lady in Montego Bay about the hospital and the conclusion we came to was the cosmetic things of the hospital is about pride. She said she would be very disappointed if one of her workers should see a piece of paper in her path coming up to the stairs to her office and ignore it.

Here are a few things I have noticed that do not require any major work or money to be spent, just the regular normal everyday work the cosmetic work that is already paid for.

a. The lights in the ceiling of the ward

b. The fans in the ceiling of the ward

c. The way the curtains are around the ward for the privacy of the patients

d. The conditions of the building outside

e. The grounds around the hospital

These are simple everyday procedures. When you look up in the ceiling of the hospital where the patients are, it seems that it has never been touched since the hospital was built. The fans are full of dust and the lights are dim because the shades seem like they have never been cleaned.

My question is, did the janitor ever change a light bulb? Or who changed the bulb? Then why can't the two things be done at the same time? Why can't the shades and the fans be cleaned? Let us get rid of the cobwebs that are so plenty.

The outside of the building, yes, it is painted nicely, but we must maintain it. I am afraid of the wasps that are living around the eaves of the building.

We have professionals that are hired at the hospital. They can figure out a way to have these simple tasks done without any disturbance to the patients.

There are so many wasps around the outside of the hospital building that the color of the eaves changed. There are so many wasp nests.

You don't have to drive into the hospital compound to see the entire wasp around the building, just look while you are passing.

The curtains around the bed for privacy, just looking at them is very depressing. The curtains are part of the hospital; it is a necessity.

They are heavily used; therefore the quality of these curtains should be more durable so that they can stand up to the wear and tear of the abuse. The amount of times that these curtains have to be replaced and the money that is spent to buy the cheap quality could be spent buying more of an industrial kind that will last longer.

There are many other little things that will make a big difference to the hospital that we are already paying to have done, so let us do it right.

I know some people might say but these are only trivial things and are not important. These are simple everyday care that will make a big difference in the appearance of the hospitals. These small things will give everyone a great feeling and would not make the hospital so run-down. All of us need to get involved. Let us start to show some pride, and let us all get involved. Jamaicans have to start thinking differently. We know that the government should provide every-thing because we all pay our tax, but truly, how many of us do pay?

This pride can go a long way. We can start by being respectful of one another. This is our first start, and things will change. Children will respect each other; children will respect parents, teachers and ministers, coworkers, and so on.

This paragraph is for returning residents and Jamaicans who are in a position to do more for the public hospitals in Jamaica. I am not saying that this group of people is not doing anything for the hospitals. I am saying that there is a lot more that can be done.

Returning residents can always go back to their country of citizen for medical treatment. We also have health insurance coverage to go to the private hospitals.

We also have the fortunate Jamaicans who can go overseas for treatments and can make arrangement for a medical ambulance to airlift them to the nearest hos-pital in Miami because they have health insurance cov-erage or they have the money.

I am not saying that anything is wrong with this kind of protection. It is a good thing to have, especially if you can afford to do it. You deserve to have it; you have worked hard for it.

I am talking about when an emergency steps into our life and the private hospitals transfer you to the public hospital. This is the critical time; the first few hours that are vital before you can get onto that air ambulance. The hospital has to do what they can do for you before you can be flown away out of Jamaica.

My research is that the private hospital will send you to the public hospital because these hospitals have the equipment to save your lives.

I wrote this paragraph because I had witnessed my dear friend survive a serious major emergency.

This emergency has opened my eyes to the major role the public hospitals, the doctors, and the nurses have played. We can have first class public hospitals in Jamaica because we already have the team that worked in the public hospitals.

I am asking that we come together and be friends of the public hospitals, and let us do more. We just don't know when we are going to need those vital few hours.

Private Hospitals

There are quite a few private hospitals in Jamaica, and most parishes have more than one. The difference with these hospitals is that you must have money to be admitted or have insurance coverage.

These hospitals provided a range of health services:

a. Accept overseas travel insurance

b. Pharmacy services are available

The cost of these private hospitals and medical centres varies.

The price to see the doctor can cost between two thousand dollars and three thousand dollars. It also depends on where in the country you are and the time of day. This payment does not involved prescription and medical test.

If you have to be admitted to the facilities, the amount of fifty thousand dollars and up is required. This amount of deposit is required before you can be admitted.

The cost of staying in the hospital is taken out of the deposit, including room and board, medication, and test. If a balance is left over prior to time of discharge, that amount is refunded to you. This amount can change depending on the time and the amount of test required.

Health Insurance

Health insurance: Jamaica has a wide range of health insurance coverage with respectable companies. The best advice is to have an agent sit with you and explain to you what coverage is best suited for you and your needs.

I believe that once you can afford to have that coverage you should definitely protect yourself.

The price also varies. It is up to you to make that decision of what is in your best interest. Remember that this is a vast amount of information so ask as much questions, take notes, and ask for pamphlets and for information so you can take home and read at your own leisure.

CHAPTER 12

Immigration and Customs

Immigration in Jamaica Traveling on a Foreign Passport

I know that I am a Jamaican by birth but lived aboard for a while. I have been living in a commonwealth country for a number of years but believed that my commonwealth passport will be valued on my return to my place of birth.

I also assumed that when I became a citizen of any of these countries I have a dual citizenship. What is the meaning of a dual citizenship from a commonwealth country? I am not talking about the USA because they are not part of the commonwealth.

So when we decided to return to Jamaica all I needed was to come home. While my husband and I was building our house, we would spend about three weeks to four months building and then back overseas.

We have never paid any attention to our passport to notice that we were stamped a visa that we were allowed to stay in the country three months. We were using the passport of the country that I am a citizen of.

On February 2010, I was returning overseas, and I was going through immigration at the Sangster International Airport. I gave the immigration officer my passport. The immigration officer told me that I have overstayed. I asked him what he meant. He said I was only allowed to stay three months.

I said to him, "I am sorry what did you say?" He repeated it. Very angrily in a state of shock, I replied to him, "What are you going to do about it? Put me in jail?" He replied, "We can do something about it next time you come to Jamaica."

The problem is that most Jamaicans would not think of another country as home. We are very grateful to that country for accepting us. We have lived there and paid our dues.

We work hard, we do the right things, we obey the laws, and overall, most of us have a very good life. We will never be ungrateful to those countries.

The fact about living in another country and becoming a citizen of that country does not mean that you are 100 percent a citizen.

The one most important thing that make you a one hundred pure citizen is being born in that country.

The fact is you can live there for one hundred years, but you are still a Jamaican. You are only a citizen of that country. I am not sounding ungrateful because we are treated with respect and that country respects our rights.

In the country that you are a citizen, the first question you are asked is, what country are you from? Never have you been asked, are you Canadian or are you British? Our very children who are born in the country are still asked the question, which country are you from?

The question that has never been asked when you are home (Jamaica) is, where are you from? The question that is asked is, which parish are you from?

The feeling that you get at the airport when you believe you are coming home is not very nice. When you joined the line that has Jamaican citizens and you have a foreign passport, you are turned away.

The immigration officer tells you to join the other lines. You have to move to another line after waiting in the first line. You have to join the other line starting at the back. After standing at the back of the line, you notice that the line is now open to all. That kind of experience is very hard to take in your place of birth.

I am asking the government of Jamaica to do something about the rules and regulations to Jamaicans who are coming home whether it is for three days, one week, one month, one year, or as a returning resident.

It is a terrible feeling when the rules and laws at the port of entry to home makes you feel like you have committed a crime.

The crime you committed is that you lived outside of Jamaica. It is a feeling that is hard to explain because if our country of birth can treat us like we are visitor, then my question is where then is home?

Immigration Leaving Jamaica

This is another puzzling question for me that I have to go through immigration leaving Jamaica. What is the reason for this the ticket agents checking my documents? I can't think of another country that I am leaving that I go through immigration, and then when I arrived in that country, I still go through immigration. The only time I can remember going through immigration is to clear immigration in the country of departure;

I will not go through immigration when I deplane. I only pick up my bags and go about my business.

Jamaica Passport Is Valued for Ten Years

I know so many Jamaicans who are coming to Jamaica using a foreign passport with an open ticket, which is for six months up to one year. This person passes through the Jamaican immigration and after leaving the airport notice that the passport is stamped three months.

The question is what is this person to do? Is this person breaking the laws of Jamaica? Should this person go to the immigration office and ask for an extension to stay in their country of birth? Or just ignore what was stamp in the passport and stay in the country of birth until it is time to leave?

If I do that, am I breaking the law, and can I be thrown in to jail for being illegal in my country of birth? I am asking the minister to give this matter some attention because I would like to know, and I believe many more Jamaicans would like to know.

I know that this person will be told that they should get a Jamaican passport or get the unlimited visa stamped in the passport. But that person does not need a Jamaican passport. They are not coming home to live in Jamaica. They only want to have an open ticket to go back when they feel like. An open ticket makes you feel free to go back when you are ready. These Jamaicans do not want to spend ten thousand Jamaican dollars for a multiple visa because they are only maybe coming home once every two years. Why is that so difficult? We are privileged to be part of the commonwealth.

The moment you are using a foreign passport, you are no longer Jamaican. I know all that, but I have a problem that passport shows that my place of birth is Jamaica. I have a foreign passport, which is part of the commonwealth, and Jamaica is part of the commonwealth.

I noticed that after the last general election in 2007 in Jamaica, there was a major problem with some of the Members of Parliament who have passport of the United States of America who has to return their citizenship of the USA if they wanted to be in the Jamaican parliament.

They could not be part of the House of Commons because USA is not part of the commonwealth. There were a lot of bye elections held in Jamaica, and the candidates have to renounce their citizenship of the USA if they wanted to be part of the election process to be in the house of parliament.

Canada is part of the Commonwealth, so why do we have a problem with a Canadian passport coming to Jamaica?

I was told we would have dual citizenship when we became Canadian citizens, and we did not lose our Jamaican citizenship.

We can be in the house of parliament in Jamaica with the Canadian passport.

These are some of the questions I have and would like answers to.

a. A tourist arrived in the country, filled out the immigration documents, and handed it to the officer along with the passport. The immigration document has a section filled out to be handed when you are leaving Jamaica. It shows the date of arrival and when you are returning—arrived November 26, 2011 and departing December 2, 2011. The immigration officer will stamp the passport February 2012. Does this tourist need to have the passport stamp with a visa for three months?

b. My husband and myself were at Toronto International Airport a few years ago checking in for our flight when the agent told us we cannot board the plane because we only have a one-way ticket to Jamaica and we are using a foreign passport. She would not check us on the flight because the policy of the Jamaican government. She told us that the policy is to fine the airline $10,000 US dollars for checking a passenger on the flight with a one-way ticket into the country.

We told the agent that we were born in Jamaica; my Canadian passport shows place of birth is Jamaica. We told her that we were not foreigners; we were born in Jamaica, so this would not affect us.

She still insisted, and she did not put us on the flight. We were told by the agent that we have to have a return ticket before she would check us on the flight.

She told us that we have to purchase a return ticket, and when we get off the flight in Jamaica, we can take the ticket to the airline desk and have the tickets refunded.

She sent us to the ticket agent; when I went to the clerk at the counter, she saw how stressed I was.

I told her the story. The first question she asked me was where I was born. I told her Jamaica. She said, "Well, I am not going to sell you a return ticket. I will come and check you in on that flight myself."

The agent told me that she will put her job on the line. "I am putting you and your husband on that flight to Jamaica." The first agent cancelled our check-in. The ticket agent checked us in on that flight.

We finally got on the flight about ten minutes before taking off. We arrived in Jamaica and no question was asked about our tickets. We put on our immigration/customs document that we were staying for one month.

When we looked at our passport, we noticed we were given three months to stay.

My question again, what is the policy? Whether we are buying our tickets online or from the travel agents, should we not be told what the policies are? Travelling is very stressful as it is, why are there so much more added to that day? Is it necessary for us to purchase a return ticket just so that when we arrive in Jamaica we can cash in that ticket? I wonder how much we would lose and what is the policy of cashing in a ticket.

Traveling to Jamaica
with My Jamaican Passport

I am now officially a Jamaican. I am on the plane to Jamaica and I am filling out the immigration forms to come home using my Jamaican passport.

The questions on the customs and immigration forms are the following:

a. How long were you out of the country?

That is a fair question, and I have no problem in answering that.

The other portion:

b. When you are returning?

Should I fill that part of the form?

I don't know. I am home. I did not fill that portion. The important thing about that part of the form is it does not matter how long you stayed in the country, you must fill that form to return once you are leave the country. I decided after about twelve months to travel overseas. I have to fill that portion of the form to present to the immigration officer because I am now using a foreign passport.

I can't travel overseas with my Jamaican passport because I need a visa to accompany my Jamaican passport, meaning I have to fill out that form?

I wrote about this subject about the immigration and customs forms because I would like to see some changes to this part of the immigration rules. I don't have to give my foreign country a form that I am leaving the country—only that when I return. "I am" asked how long I have been out of the country.

The other question is that why can't one immigration/customs card used per household? Is it necessary for each person to fill a card? All that we have to do is add the names. They are all the same address. The Jamaican government doesn't notice how much money is wasted for all this paperwork. This is one way to save.

In the process of writing this manuscript, I travelled overseas, and I had a candied talk with the immigration officer and told her that I am so confused with the process of the immigration rules, and this is what she told me to do to help me with the process.

a. When I am travelling from overseas to Jamaica, fill out the immigration forms. As for the portion for returning, leave the date for returning blank.

b. When you are going overseas, hand in the foreign passport and the Jamaican passport with the return slips and the return date filled out with the date of departure to the immigration officer.

I will do that next time that I am travelling out of the country but still I am questioning the process of why.

I have complained a bit about the process of the passport and the forms, but I have a bit of good news that I'm sharing because this is what this book is about: the good and the bad of my experience about coming home. On my way home from my trip overseas, I noticed a breath of fresh air when I arrived at immigration at Sangster International.

It was twelve noon and about five airplanes arrived one after the other. There was about one thousand passengers to clear immigration when I noticed an overhead sign that read Jamaican citizen to go to that line. I went over, stood in that line, and was called. I handed my Jamaican passport, cleared immigration, and was out within five minutes. This is my bit of good news that there is privilege of owning a Jamaican passport.

Customs

After landing at the airport and you clear immigration, you still have another hurdle to go through before you reached freedom. The next stop is to clear customs, and then you have to go to get your luggage and load them on to a cart. I am not complaining about that process, my complaint is that without any help I have to get my bags and put them on the cart.

I have to push the cart with my bags to customs; you alone have to take off the bags from the cart to put on the customs table.

Customs inspected your luggage, then fine you or let you free. Then you alone have to pack up your luggage then lift them back on to the cart. Then push the cart to the door. Then you are told you can't go any further with the cart. You are told that your luggage must be taken outside by a porter.

Let me say something to the system and policy of the airport; this is wrong. This is terribly unfair. If I am going to pay for a porter, let the porter do the work.

How is it that I alone do all the work inside customs, yet I have to pay for my luggage to be taken outside just a very short distance of about fifteen feet?

What is this about? I don't have a problem with the government trying to find ways to put more Jamaicans to work. I am also willing to pay the full amount and even to give something extra. I get it. I understand it very well, but here is my problem. I cannot understand why I have to do all the work inside and the last little bit I can't do myself.

I am told I have to get a porter to take the luggage outside.

I would like also to say something, if you want to see that people are not happy about the system, stand outside at arrival and see how many people are coming out without porters. These people are taking out the luggage themselves.

I will also make a comment that most of the airlines have changed their policy. They are charging passengers to check in luggage or for a second luggage. Most passengers are now travelling with one piece of luggage. The passengers of today are travelling light, and they are taking their luggage themselves outside.

Shipping a Barrel

Shipping a barrel or two to Jamaica is so easy. All you do is shop, pack your barrel, call the shipping company, and they come and give you the shipping documents then you pay the cost of shipping.

Collecting Your Barrel

Jamaica is now the problem. The headache started when the expensive phone call comes. A broker calls to let you know that your shipment is here, and they give you the address to come and pick up the documents, and you have to pay fifteen hundred dollars to process the documents.

The next journey is to the wharf where you have to see about three different departments before your barrel is opened.

The barrel is opened for the customs officer and next is the cashier where you pay the duty that is assigned. You now have to pay the person who takes the barrel from the back for the customs officers who opens and closes the barrel.

The next payment is for another person who is to take the barrel outside to put on the vehicle. The process of shipping a barrel to Jamaica has to go through so many procedures it can be very stressful and costly.

The conclusion you come to is that you are discouraged because they don't want you to bring anything to Jamaica.

I do not have a problem with the government trying to find work for the people. But why is the whole process costing so much money? The questions I would like to have answered are the following:

a. Are the workers who brings the barrels from the back to the front to be opened and inspected by the customs officer being paid by the government?

b. Why do we have to pay another set of workers to take the barrels outside?

c. Are the workers who take the barrels from inside the building and put it on the vehicles employees of the government?

So if you total the cost of shipping a barrel from overseas, you pay the cost from the shipper to the broker, then the charges to the government, and then the duty again to the government, to the two men, and to the vehicle for the destination.

The next question I would like to know is if there is a different price to clear a barrel through customs if you ship a barrel to yourself from overseas and them come to Jamaica to clear customs or if the barrel is shipped to a relative to be picked up?

The reason for this question is because of two instances about two ladies; one lives in Jamaica who was visiting her family overseas and spent a month. The other lady lives in Canada and came home for a family reunion; they both each have five barrels. They have the basic things like food, clothes, the odd things maybe a kettle or toaster and so forth.

The only difference in the barrels is that the lady who lives in Canada has two small televisions in her barrel. You can just image how small these televisions are because they are in a barrel. There was a big difference for the customs charges for these barrels; the lady from Canada paid one hundred and forty thousand dollars while the lady who lives in Jamaica paid twenty-five thousand dollars. What could be in those barrels to cost that amount of money?

My question is, is it worth it to ship a barrel to Jamaica? We are not even talking about the fact that you have to plan to spend a day.

Is there a plan for Jamaicans not to send any barrels home? But then look at how many jobs depended on shipping a barrel.

Would we be better off to just forget all the hassle and just give to the family members the money and let them do what they want to do with it.

A few years ago, I airfreighted a box with some window blinds to Montego Bay airport.

I packed the box with the blinds but used some of my used clothes to pack the box so that the blinds would not be damaged. I should have used newspaper or plastic because a value was put on my used clothes, and I was charged a duty.

If you airfreight any goods to Jamaica, you have to itemize each item and provide a proof of receipt.

Shipping of a Container

The following are requirements for shipping a container for returning residents:

a. You must have a list of each items in the container

b. Receipts for all the new items in the container.

c. Documents showing that you have been living overseas. It could be a bill payment in your name or a tax receipt.

These documents have to be taken to the tax department for returning residents.

The most important thing to do before you send that container is to visit the Jamaican Consulate Office in the city you are living.

A visit to that office will provide you with valuable information to make shipping of your container as stress free as possible. Also remember that that all these government agencies all have a website.

Motor Vehicle

Shipping a motor vehicle to Jamaica is a very expensive venture to take on. There is a lot of paperwork and cost attached to such venture. Jamaica has all the vehicles or almost all the vehicles that you can think of. You will save yourself a lot of stress if you go into a dealer here in Jamaica and buy yourself a vehicle.

It might seem a lot of money to buy the vehicle here because you have your vehicle at home and you just want to bring it home.

The taxes are very exuberant to bring the vehicle into Jamaica with all the shipping cost and all the other expenses you will encounter. You can imagine the stress. Just imagine the frustrations to ship and clear the container of the vehicle.

The choice is also yours if you decide to ship your vehicle to Jamaica. Make sure before you make that decision to proceed that you have all the valued information and visit the Jamaican consulate office in the city you are or the nearest office. Remember a visit to this office will prevent a lot of headache if you are shipping a vehicle to Jamaica.

Shipping this vehicle required a lot of paperwork. To the shipper, remember you are paying a lot of duty on that vehicle. My advised is to visit a car dealer hear in Jamaica before you start the process of bringing in a motor vehicle.

Jamaican Passport

After the constant harassment coming into Jamaica with my foreign passport, I decided to get my Jamaican passport. This Jamaican passport can only be used to come into Jamaica. This passport cannot be used to enter any other country; you must have a visa to accompany it.

Anyway, our journey to get our passport begun; this was my first encounter in Jamaica about dress code. (See the chapter on dress code.)

I filled out the application form along with the passport pictures and went to see a justice of the peace to have the document and pictures signed and seal. The next day, I went to the passport office properly dressed with everything covered.

I went inside without the security stopping me from entering, took my seat, and waited for my turn. I handed my documents to the passport agent, and she looked over the document.

The agent turned to me and told me that the justice of the peace should not have signed all the pictures; the reason is that the ink from the pen with the signature will show up in the passport. These pictures are no longer of value. I have to retake the pictures over and bring them back to her without the signature.

She will use the ones she wanted signed from the first batch and the rest from the unsigned ones.

The first question I asked was, why was this information not given somewhere either to the justice of the peace or were we get the application forms?

My other problem was the passport that I was issued over thirty-seven years ago. I had no idea where the passport was.

I know that it was not stolen, and I did not lose it. Just don't know where it is. I was now told that I have to report the passport lost to the police and make a report. The cost for this report is seven thousand dollars. After the report, I had to bring that report to the passport office.

The other problem I have is my name. My maiden name is on my birth certificate; my other passport has my married name. I was just in the process of changing my other documents to my new married name. The passport office wanted me to show them a copy of my divorce papers. To show that I am the same persons I say I am.

The problem I have with this conversation is that I have never been asked to show any document to prove what my name is, not even my birth certificate. The only document I have ever had to prove that this is my new name is my marriage certificate.

I told the clerk I have no idea where those documents are. I had been divorced over twenty years ago, and I have never had to present them for any reason. I have now moved to Jamaica, and most of those papers are shredded. I was sent packing with the folder, and if I wanted to have a Jamaican passport, these are the requirements.

The other choice I had if I want to be free to come and go in Jamaica without any problem at the airport, now that I have my house in Jamaica, is to pay ten thousand dollars to have an unlimited visa stamp in the foreign passport.

I left the passport office very disappointed wondering how I am going to get a Jamaican passport. I could go on the Internet and do a search, but my problem was that I had no record of the date of my first marriage. I could recall the month and year but not the day.

I went home and called my family to ask them if they have any memory of the day I got married the first time. Unfortunately, no one could recall that date. I tried to do the search but with no success.

A week went by, and I was talking to my cousin who lives in Kingston. I was telling her the problem I had getting my passport. She asked me why I not call the Kingston office. The next day bright and early I called the passport office in Kingston. I spoke to a customer service agent; I must have hit the jackpot that day because of this young lady. I changed her name; I will call her Beverly. I told Beverly my problems.

I told her how stressed and burdened I am; I talked to her about everything I could complain about. I told Beverly all the documents that I have and I still could have a justice of the peace to verify who I say I am because he taught me in school. After pouring my heart out and telling her how frustrated I am. Beverly said to me, "You have enough documents for you to get your passport."

I said to her, "Then what is the matter with this agent? Why can't she process my document so I can get my passport?"

Beverly said to me that I am to come into Kingston, she would process the passport and she could get my passport within twenty-four hours.

I told her I don't know much about Kingston, and I don't wish to travel to the Kingston's office when we have the same office here in Montego Bay. I asked her if she could call the supervisor in the Montego Bay office to help me to process the documents.

Her reply was it is much better for me to come in that office and I can have the process done immediately. I told her if that is the only way for me to get my passport then I will come into the office the next day.

A few minutes after I hung up the phone, I started thinking about the conversation I just had. I am thinking if Beverly is saying that the documents I have were enough information for me to have my passport processed, then I am going to the Montego Bay office to speak to a supervisor.

I called my husband and told him we are going to the passport office in Montego Bay. We went to the office with my folder again, following the dress code, and went in, took my seat, and waited my turn.

It must be my lucky day, or I am heading for a disaster on this day because my turn was next, and I am going to see the same agent who told me that I could not have my passport process with these documents.

How lucky of a day because nothing has changed in the file. I smiled, took my seat, and said to her, "I don't know if you remember me. I was here a week ago. I am back and lucky me I have the pleasure of having you as my agent again. I also have to tell you that nothing has changed in the file. The documents are the same. The other documents you asked me for, I don't have them, and I can't get them."

I told her I am here to see a supervisor because I spoke to a supervisor in the Kingston office, her name is Beverly, and she told me I have enough documents to have my documents process. She took the folder from me and looked them over again, then turned to me and said she must be sleeping the day when I came to her because, yes, I had the proper documents to process the passport.

I took a deep breath and just listened for the next instruction. She told me to go upstairs, see an immigration police, report the lost passport, and they will give me a letter to take back to her. I went upstairs and gave them the information about my lost passport. I paid the seven thousand dollars then was given a sealed envelope of which I took downstairs to the agent.

The documents were processed. I paid the cost for the passport and was given a receipt and that someone will call me to come and pick up my passport.

The experience about my passport is this. When the Jamaican government gives you a passport, remember one thing, it is not your property; and as long as you live, it is the property of the Jamaica government.

The important thing to know is that once you decide to come home, these documents are very important in Jamaica like any other country. The question is this: I have all the documents to process these papers. Then why is it so difficult and frustrating to have them processed? I wonder about the other citizens who do not have as much of the documents that I have.

The documents that I have were valued documents that I have been using for thirty-seven years in a foreign country with over thirty million people. And these documents were not appropriate document to be used in Jamaica.

My question is this: Why is it so difficult to obtain these documents even when you have legal papers to back up who you are?

I will say one thing after the journey of going through the process of getting my passport and my birth certificate. A lot of the process is surely not necessary; it can be done in a much easier way. It is about time we have more respect for the citizens of this country.

The agent who is sitting across from the citizen needs to listen more, help more, and stop the attitude of not treating the citizen with respect—it would make a huge difference.

On January 30, 2012, at 8:30 in the evening, I was at home when my niece told me she was going to the police station to pick up a report for a lost passport because she is getting her Jamaican passport. I told her that she did not have to do that; she could just go to Overton Plaza at the immigration office in Montego

Bay and report the lost passport to the immigration police upstairs the passport office.

There is cost of either seven thousand dollars or ten thousand dollars; I don't remember how much I paid. My niece said to me, "But I am not paying any money for the letter from the police."

My Jamaican passport was issued in June 2010. As far as my passport is concerned, it was done, it was finished and over, and I promised that I would not lose this passport again. It is now January 2012. This is a bit of information provided so that what happened to me will not happen to anyone. Please do not pay anyone to replace a lost or stolen passport. I was in a state of shock because I paid the immigration police officer ten thousand dollars for me to get this letter for the new passport to be issued. The next morning, at about 9:30 a.m., I called the passport office and asked to speak to a supervisor. I told him who I was and the reason why I am calling.

The supervisor told me that it is not the normal procedure for the lost passport to reported upstairs at that office. The report is to be made at a police station. I told him that I was told to go upstairs and give the information about the lost passport. He asked me who the officer was; I told him I have no recollection of his name, but maybe if I see him in person I could remember him.

The supervisor asked me for receipt of the payment. I told him I will have to look for the receipt. I told the supervisor that he was in a position to look back at the report and see who the officer was who signed the document; he told me the documents are in the archive in Kingston.

The passport was issued June 2010, and it is now January 2012. How difficult is it for the document to get from the archive? The supervisor told me that he was going to transfer the call to the police immigration department because there was a corporal who was in that department who will remember who took the information from me that day. I told the corporal the conversation that took place when I was asked to pay the money.

I told the officer, "I can't understand why I have to pay so much money to get a Jamaican passport when the passport is only valued in Jamaica. If I had to used that passport to enter in any other country, I would have to have a visa to accompany that passport."

The conversation did not go very well between the supervisor and the corporal; I was accused of making up stories, and I did not pay for the report.

The interesting thing about this conversation was that I was not even aware of what had happened to me—that I paid for a passport that I should not have been paid for.

The conversation was finished with the corporal telling me he would get back to me. I have learned so much from this process because I believe in the system and also believe in the process. I did not take home the sealed envelope with me; it was given to the agent. The mistake that I made is that I have no names of the officers who I spoke to or who wrote the report of my lost passport.

I wrote my story, and you see the end result of each story is a different story. I believe that after going through the system and the difficulties, I can say a few things. I have valued documents from overseas that I have used for so many years. Documents with a photograph of me with my name and date of birth that corresponded with my birth certificate and these were not enough.

Then how about the people who do not have any document to back up what they are saying?

The stress that one has to tolerate to get the basic documents can be so much easier. When you listen to the talk shows, the frustration from the people is unbearable.

I believe better can be done, and I hope that the people who are in charge will start thinking about the people of Jamaica. Let's make the citizens' of Jamaica feel that when they walk into a government office that they are coming in for help to fix something that is a problem.

The first start to this process is for the government workers to listen to the people and respect them when they walk in. The feeling of making the citizens feel stupid and not worthy because you are sitting in that chair and what you say is the law is the kind unacceptable behaviour; the employees that the public have to encounter need to be more polite and respectful.

The other lesson I have learned through this process is this: please keep all your records and receipts. The other thing is to only pay a cashier when dealing with any government agency. The other thing is do not take anything for granted. If your gut feeling is that something is wrong, stop and ask questions because most likely something is wrong.

This is what I have observed through my journey in Jamaica. When you check into a hotel in Jamaica, you feel that you are not in Jamaica. You could never be in Jamaica; there is respect from the moment you enter that compound. There is a smile; there is a hello.

I am just in awe when I am in a hotel in Jamaica with the customer service and the kindness. I have always asked myself how much money these workers are paid; they are in such good moods, and they are so friendly. I am always so inquisitive; I would ask them how much they are being paid.

The question is not about the money because they are not been paid a big salary. It is not that they love their job so much that, yes, they are happy and that they have a job to put food on the table. I believe that it is about training, so if we can get that kind of service in the hotel, they why has the service stop there?

Why then are we not getting respect from each other when we enter into a government office? Or in other businesses, why has customer service not continued? What is with this attitude that we can't have it right across the board?

There are so many tourists that I know that have stayed at these resorts and asked me about the workers at these resorts and how come they are so polite and happy.

They can hear them singing, very pleasant, and always have a smile on their faces. What is it? They want to know how much the workers are making or if Jamaicans are just happy because they have a job.

I wish I could answer those questions because I attend a meeting once a week at one of these resorts, and I too noticed the difference. I wonder what it is between the hotel workers and the government workers. I know for sure it is not the money because the government workers are paid more than the workers at the resorts. So what is it that makes the difference? I am going to assume that because they are dealing with Jamaicans we do not have to be polite. The other reason is, whether it is the store or the cashier, the money is not available to train the workers in customer service.

Birth Certificate

Getting My Son's Birth Certificate

This story is about me getting a copy of my son's birth certificate. My son lost his birth certificate. He decided to try online but was not able to get anywhere with that process. We decided on a trip to Jamaica; we will start the process to get a copy. We decided to go into Spanish Town to start the process; that was not a pleasant day.

My son's birth certificate was issued in 1970. According to the clerk, so many things was wrong with that birth certificate. His father's name was on the birth certificate, but he did not sign the birth certificate; my name was on it, but I did not sign the birth certificate. It was my mother who registered my son, so of course, she signed the birth certificate.

I was given a sealed envelope to be taken back to the district of Askenish in the parish of Hanover where he was registered. I am to hand the envelope to the clerk to reregister the birth. Once the postmistress registered the birth, I will received a sealed envelope of which I must return within twenty-four hours back to Spanish Town.

I asked her if I could send it by courier to the registrar office. She told me in a stern voice, no, it must be hand delivered.

I came back to Hanover and started calling the number. I was directed all over the place until finally I was in touch with the postmistress all the way in Green Island; I told her what I have to do.

She is now working at more than one post office, so she told me she will be at this location the next day, and she will bring the book for that area so I could come the next day.

The following day, I drove to Green Island in the parish of Hanover, went to the post office, and handed the postmistress the sealed envelope. She took her book and wrote the information. I paid the charges and took the sealed envelope and drove to Spanish Town.

I took the envelope to the floor, waited my turn, then when I was called, handed the envelope to the clerk. The clerk told me the cost and asked me what service I needed; I paid for the service and walked out the door.

My son's new birth certificate does not have his father's name on it; they did not ask for his father's information. His father is deceased.

This Is the Story of Getting My Birth Certificate

I could tell you many more stories about what a nightmare it is to get your Jamaican birth certificate. The problem is that the government is trying to make sure that every Jamaican has a birth certificate.

The problem is that before the government tried to solve that part of making sure we are all registered, they tell you that the first birth certificate you have is not valued anymore, and you need a new one.

One early morning, we decided to go the registrar office in Montego Bay, which is the closest location for us. We took a number and had a seat. The first thing I noticed was that we were not allowed to drink water inside this area; you have to go outside to drink the water.

While we were sitting there, a young lady came and sat beside us. She asked us what numbers we have; I showed her the numbers. She said she noticed I had been waiting for quite a while, then she said to take these numbers and I was now moved up ten places.

We took the numbers from her and gave her our numbers. Our numbers was called; we went and sat in front of the agent. I gave her my particulars about my birth certificate.

After a few seconds, I was told that my birth certificate was not on the system. I said to her I have ten brothers and sisters and asked if they were on the computer. She said yes.

I said to her that this is strange because I have a birth certificate with my parents' names on it and my name also. I just don't have it with me and that the old birth certificate is not valued anymore; I am getting a new one.

The agent told me I had to pay for a search, and the cost is one hundred dollars. My husband was told the same. My husband was not surprised because he knew that there was some complication with his birth certificate.

I was caught off guard when she told me that I was not in the system. I went to another area, and I paid the money to have the search done, and I was given a receipt. Two days after, I received a phone call from a clerk from Spanish Town to inform me that there was no record of my birth certificate and that I have to go back to the Montego Bay office to apply for a late registration.

I went, took my number, and waited my turn. The clerk gave me some documents.

a. I need a copy of my school-registered paper.

b. I need a document for the justice of the peace to sign and have him seal it.

c. I have to have an older sibling register me, and I have to go to the justice of the peace to witness the signatures.

I am fifty-eight years old and not able to reregister myself. I need an older sibling to register me.

I telephoned my schoolmate who is a teacher at the school I attended and asked her about my school record and if she could get them for me. I then called my elderly sister who lives in Lucea and told her my problem and that I would like her to accompany me to the registration office to register me for my birth certificate.

If she agreed, she will have to close her business by 2:00 p.m. because she also will have to go a justice of the peace to have the documents signed and sealed and to be in Montego Bay before the office closed at 4:30 p.m.

All kind of things started to spin around in my head. I am from a family of sixteen children. Four siblings have passed away; my brother, who I follow, is supposed to be two years older than I am, but the school record is now showing that he is only one year older than I am.

I started to think all different things now that my parents are deceased. I have no one to turn to for answers to my questions. I started to think that the father that I know and love was not on my birth certificate in Spanish Town. As for the old one I have, where did my mother get that birth certificate from with my dad's name on it? I could get my pension a year earlier, and I wasted a year that I can't get back.

After a very confusing night where I could not sleep, the next day before I drove to Hanover, I drove to the registration office to ask them if I will be served if I showed up at the door at least fifteen minutes before closing time just in case the traffic is a problem coming into Montego Bay from Lucea. The reply was that they will serve me.

I drove to my school in Clifton and picked up my school records. I looked at the school records and noticed a major problem. My school record was showing that I was one year older. My birth certificate that

I have used all my life according to my school record is wrong.

I went to my sister's place of business and took her to the address of the Justice of the Peace. The Justice of the Peace witnessed my sister's signature, filled out the forms, signed them, and then used his seal to stamp the documents. We then drove to Montego Bay to get to the registration office before they closed.

I walked in and took a number and waited my turn. Then when I went to the clerk, it was my lucky evening; I got the same clerk who told me that my name was not in the system. We sat down, my sister and myself, and I put the folder on the desk with my hand on it. I turned to her and I said to her, "Today is my lucky day because I have you again."

I asked very nicely and kindly that before she opened the file that I would like to ask her two questions. I said to her that I was told that a birth certificate is in Spanish Town.

I asked her if she could let me know the date of birth that is on that birth certificate because my school records is showing that I am a year older, and I explained to her about the birth certificate that I have been using. I told her that I have lost out on one year of my pension.

The problem I have is that if they are going to use my school records to give me a new birth certificate, I now have to change all these documents to correspond with my new birth certificate. I am going to have all kind of confusion just to change them. It is going to show that I am a fraud because I lied on my birth certificate.

The next question I had for her is if I could tell her the name of the brother I followed, and according to my school record, he is only one year older than me, and he has my father's name. I also have my older sibling with me who is the fourth child and have my father's name, and she is going to register me. I also have a copy of my youngest brother's birth certificate with my father's name on the birth certificate.

If you look in the computer, you will see eleven children, one mother, and one father. My parents married when my mother was fifteen and my father was twenty-one. My father died at seventy-two years old and my mother at eighty-six years old.

The clerk, after listening to my story, said to me, "You are right. Something did not make sense." She said to me, "Please excuse me for a second. I am going to make a phone call to Spanish Town." The clerk gave the person at the other end a code; within fifteen seconds, she came off the telephone and told me that my birth certificate is in Spanish Town.

The clerk gave me a paper to take to the cashier's desk to pay for my birth certificate. I was asked what service I wanted: one month or seven days. I chose seven days. I paid for seven days but received it in one month. It does not matter how little the cost is; respect the fact that you asked me to pay for a service, and you must honour it.

The government need to respect the service just like how they need to respect their citizens. This is one simple area we can start with: the registrar's office. Don't just take the money and not provide the service.

When I was in the process of applying for my birth certificate, I was told by a friend to not pay for the service for seven days because I was not going to get it in seven days.

This is a citizen telling me how rotten the system is and not to waste my money because the government will only take my money, and I will not get the service I paid for.

These are just some of the simple areas where our government can start: don't offer a service that you can't honor. If the agency cannot offer seven days within Montego Bay but can offer it in Kingston, then don't offer the service for Montego Bay and offer it only for Kingston.

There are so many reasons why the government needs to respect the service they offer.

When you offer me the seven day service based on this information, I have planned to go overseas. I had to travel without my birth certificate.

If I needed this document to be used for something overseas, I would have to make another trip.

The question that I have with all of this painful experience is what happens to the people who are not lucky to get a listening ear. Those people who cannot speak for themselves. The experience was very painful—a lot of time consumed and money spent that was not necessary. Not to mention the cost to my sister who had to close her business for the afternoon. A lot of time and gas was spent to drive to get her and the time to take her to Montego Bay and to drive her back to Lucea. I believe that there must be an easier way for it to be done. If the justice of the peace used a seal and witnessed the signature and it is a document from the registrar's office, why was that not sufficient? Why did I have to have my sister in person?

Does this mean you have doubts in the seal of the justice of the peace that is appointed by the government? Should that seal be something of honor when it is stamped on a document by a justice of the peace?

It seems that we have to add extra frustration into almost everything we have to do. Does that mean even though we have the system in place we do not trust the system? Why can't things be simpler?

There is also a system in Montego Bay in regard to your passport and birth certificate that there are agents who can work for you to process these documents so you do not have to have the stress and frustration that comes along with processing these papers. Therefore, you pay for these documents twice. The agents who do the work have to be paid and you pay for the documents to be processed.

CHAPTER 13

Utilities

Jamaica Public Service

The first encounter with the Jamaica Public Service Company is when we make the application for electricity while we were in the process of building our house. We applied for the permit for us to have electricity on our premises. We received a letter stating that for us to have access to electricity the cost will be five hundred thousand Jamaican dollars ($500,000). This payment is non-refundable.

The street we were building the house on was only about three blocks (three lots) from the last house. My husband and I were a bit taken aback for the amount and that it is nonrefundable.

We called the office and asked about the letter we received, and we were told to appeal the letter. We also made an appointment to see the manager. On the day of the appointment, we had a lot of questions.

a. The first question we had was we are at lot number six and there are about three other lots before our lot and many after our lot. When the other land owners decided to build, where is the electricity coming from to service their lots?

b. Because you are asking for that much money and it is nonrefundable, then the electricity should be our private electric current.

c. If the JPS is supplying the service from my private service, then why not give back the money as each new application is made?

d. If they are charging us to run the electricity along the road to our house and the money is nonrefundable, I am assuming that it is ours distinctively.

The meeting finished with me telling the manager that I will use a generator until the JPS run the wire or stop building and go back to my country of citizenship.

We left the office and went downstairs where we parked, and just as we were about to go into the vehicle, my cell phone rang. It was the manager from the JPS that we had just wrapped up the meeting with.

He asked us if we could meet him at the location. We went to the lot and waited for him; he came with an engineer and two other men. I left and did not attend the meeting while they were walking up and down the street.

The meeting with all these men took about thirty minutes to complete. The manager told us he will get back in touch with us shortly.

The letter came to us about two weeks after with the context of the letter changed. The amount of nonrefundable money we will pay was one hundred thousand dollars.

We had to try every possible source to get the streetlight up and running. I could write a complete chapter on streetlights, but I do not want to at this time. I will save that for the next book. This part of the deal I got in Jamaica I am going to take this one with a grain of salt and swallow with plenty water.

Power Outage

The other thing we did not know about was power outages; we did not know that when you have power outage you must call to report and give the location.

I have been living in a country for over thirty-seven years and never had to call if and when we have a power outage. I come home with the same attitude of waiting for the power to be automatically fixed. The street we live on only about six houses, a school, a church, and a community centre. The school is closed on the weekend, and the church most of the time is only active on a Sunday and the community centre is only active if there is a function.

Most of the people also on the street still travel back and forth overseas. I waited over twelve hours one Sunday for electricity to be restored.

The problem is that it was only my street on that day, and the people on that street were not home. We learned from that day that you must call and make a report; don't depend on someone else to call.

Air conditioning: Because of the climate, you think of air-conditioning in your house when planning to return to Jamaica. It is very important on how your house is designed. If you are thinking of an open concept, you are thinking of central air-conditioning. You need to take another look on that decision.

The problem with that concept is that electricity is extremely expensive, and you will pay dearly for such a concept. It also depends on the size of your house when you are thinking about central air-conditioning.

Another thing you are to make sure of is that your stove for cooking is not electricity. The concept that we are used to from overseas is not the ideal thing for Jamaica. Cooking with gas is the best concept for this country especially how often we have power failure.

You would have to be very rich if you were to find yourself in the position to use electricity to cook, to iron, air-condition, to wash, to dry, to have hot water and for the radio, the television, the fridge, and the freezer working constantly, to bake and the light around the house is on all night.

You could find yourself in the range of over forty to fifty thousand dollars or more per month. The customers are demonstrating against the high cost of their bills and how could it be so expensive when all they have is a fridge, a television, an iron, and a radio and the light in the house.

The electricity can be a tricky situation; some customers complain about damages to their appliances. There are times when you do not get enough electricity to maintain all that is required to run the household. You have to call the JPS and let them know the problem you are having.

The problems started with some parts of the house. Some are without current and you do not have any of your fuse chip. The fridge is not working properly because it is not getting enough current. The gate opener is not working, so you have to open the gate manual.

Be prepared when you call or report a power failure for you will be told it will take about five to six hours for service to be restored.

The problem it is so important that we must have electricity is because of our security that is connected to our telephone. If you have a power outage, then your security is not functioning.

I will give you an example of what the cost of electricity can cause. This story will explain how expensive it is to do anything extra except the normal everyday function.

I am telling this story because it is almost five days before Christmas 2011. When I first came to the area where I am living during the Christmas season, there were lots of lights all over the area. It was a pleasure when you drive around to see all the decorations and lights.

A lot of houses were decorated, the lights were pretty, and the festive season was around the community. As the years go by, you noticed the difference with the decorations and lights; they are fewer and fewer.

It got worse each year, so far it seems as if there will not be any decorations at all this year. Adding lights for your Christmas decoration to your already high cost of electricity can make a big difference in your electricity bill in one month. This is Christmas 2011. I was right about the festive seasons; there were no lights in my neighbourhood.

Water

I must state that the water in Jamaica is very good drinking water. I thoroughly enjoy drinking the water more than any bottled water in Jamaica.

I don't know what departments control what areas in regard to water in Jamaica, but there is a serious problem with the way water is used and respected in Jamaica.

The important thing is to make sure you have access to water where you are building, and even when you have access, make sure you have backup; you can't totally depend on this system. One good thing about Jamaica is that there is a lot of rainfall sometimes.

If you have a system to collect the rainwater and store it, you could use that water for all the gardening, washing of the vehicles, and all the activities outside. You are saving the environment because that water has no chemicals.

The other important thing is that you are saving money because your water bill is less, so it is a good thing all around.

The other problem about water in Jamaica is when you listen to the talk shows. The citizens are calling to beg the host to ask the water department to get some water for the community. Some of these neighbour-hoods have no water for many years; water is a very important commodity.

I can hear all these pleas but then you will drive pass a water pipe broken for weeks; the water is wasting many gallons just running down the gully.

I always wonder if no one cares or because no one called to report these broken pipes.

I came to the conclusion that it is not that the citizens who don't care because they do call the water department, but the water commission does not care or they do not have the parts to fix the problem, so the water is wasted until such time.

I have seen water pipes broken, and I have called every number that I could dial. I talked to everyone that I could talk to and reported the broken water pipe. It took over one month for the broken water pipe to be fixed.

There are so many people who cannot get water, yet you see water constantly being wasted. This is very sad because I lived in a country for over thirty years, and there is so much respect for water. I am very concerned when I see the water wasted.

Solid Waste Management Agent

Collecting of Solid Waste

After over six years of trying everything in our powers to have our waste collected, we have failed. We have contacted the solid waste management department and spoken to each and every one from the person in charge at the top to the truck driver.

We still cannot get any response of picking up our waste. We have had a lot of promises, and finally, we were told that the road is in terrible condition, and they are not able to drive to pick up the waste. I have come to the conclusion about my garbage collection.

I have three choices with the garbage:

a. Burn the garbage:

I cannot burn the garbage because the smell of the burnt garbage makes me sick.

b. Throw the garbage over the gully:

I could throw the garbage on the other side of the road in front of my house and let the garbage wash down to the bottom of the road till it gets to the sea. But my conscience will not allow me to do that.

c. The last one is to find someone in the neighbourhood to help:

My husband has asked someone in the neighbourhood if he could put the garbage in their bin for collection.

We now put the waste in our vehicle and drive it to the neighbour down the street twice per week. While I was writing the book, my husband set himself a task to have the road fixed. The road is now completed; our next task is to try and have the solid waste management to collect our waste.

Roads

On buying our property, we were told that the road was going to be fixed and that the money was in place. We now have the land for about five years, and we started to ask about the road; we were still getting the same answer.

This is it. We were now in a jam because we are now ready to build, and the road is in worse condition because of the constant rainfall washing away the little that is left. We are now ready to have the trucks bring material to start building the house. We started to fix the potholes so that the truck can bring the material.

We now have to bring in truckloads of marl to fix the road to drive to our house. After about three years, we got the news we were waiting for: the fixing of the road has started.

The problem with the new road was that, yes, the road was started, but started from the other end and they worked all the way to about twenty yards from my gate and stopped.

It is now six years, and we have not seen anyone come to do anything about the road.

We have no road to drive to our property, but we have been constantly trying our best to cover the road by using concrete or gravel.

The interesting thing about this road is that it is a public road, and when my husband pays people to help him to spread the asphalt, not one driver would stop to help him to work on the road that they are driving on.

This is a conversation my husband had with a man who drives a truck on the road every day.

My husband asked him how much it would cost if he is to bring a few loads of marl to put on the road. He told my husband ten thousand dollars per load. My husband said to him, "But we are all driving on the road. Let us all come together and fix the road so that we could drive and save our vehicles from all the repairs it is costing us every week."

He said, "No, let the government fix it," and that was the end of the conversation. We have tried everything in our powers to get some work done on the road.

My husband has been trying for the last six years to fix the road, but every time we fix it, the rain will wash it away. The problem is that we cannot dig any drain on the road. But he has been using other materials now instead of the marl for it to last a little longer.

We have been fixing the road from the other end coming toward our gate. The road towards our gate is now completed, and the motorists are now enjoying the beauty of driving towards our gate. The road after our gate is in such terrible condition that the vehicles are having a hard time driving toward the other end.

The people have to get out of the vehicle and push the vehicle for it to pass this area. The passenger in the vehicle most of the time has to get out of the vehicle and walk so that the vehicle can drive to a better area, and they will walk toward the vehicle.

A few weeks ago, the very same man whom my husband had asked to bring some marl to put on the road came to my husband and asked him if he could also fix the road past our gate. I believe that this man might think that we are the government and that we are collecting his tax.

The maintenance to our vehicle is a tremendous cost to us every month. We asked the other drivers to help with the road and they told us it is not their responsibility, but the government's.

The good news is that we were finally able to fix the road to a point now that we, our friends, and our family can drive a little better coming to our house. The general public now has a road to take them anywhere they want to go. I must give a lot of credit to my husband. The journey was very difficult; many times the pain was so severe after spreading the asphalt on the road. The interesting thing about all of this is that many times he is driving past a latest model vehicle, they are ready to push him off the road because they are to be in the best part of the road not knowing that this road was fixed all from our pocket and not the government's.

Property Taxes in Jamaica

I am a returning resident, and after living overseas for over thirty-seven years, I know that the property tax is to make sure we have road, water, hospital, garbage collections, schools, and security.

I also know that we do not pay the amount of property tax that we pay overseas, but since I have been here, my property taxes has gone up almost seventy-five percent.

What have I got for my property tax? Nothing. No road, no garbage collection. I have not seen any improvement in the hospital and no improvement in the road. I have not seen any improvement in absolutely anything.

I have called the members of Parliament, I have attended meetings, and I have joined the neighbourhood watch. I have attended the mayor's forum. I have called the waste management agent. It is now over six years and still I have not received any response to any of my pleas.

Good News

During the time of writing this book, some good news
emerged. I am now having a great relationship with the
councillor for the area. I can tell you things are so much
better. I know for sure when I discussed with him about
the solid waste management that I will have something
done. The other good news is that a fund raising drive
is in effect for the Cornwall Regional Hospital and I
hope that every person who reads this book will con-
tribute to this drive.

CHAPTER 14

Dress Code in Jamaica

Did you know that Jamaica has a dress code, and it is a very active law?

These are some of the places where dress code is active:

- Hospitals
- Passport office
- Correctional facilities
- Schools
- Church
- The photographs for the passport

For the photographs that you have to take for the passport picture, you cannot wear sleeveless.

One of the first things that greet you on a visit to some government offices is the dress code; the rules stipulate how you should dress to enter. This is a strict code to which you must comply adhere before entering.

Jamaica temperature is always up to eighty degrees Fahrenheit or more.

My first experience with dress code in Jamaica was the passport office in Montego Bay to start the process of getting our passport. We went to the office to pick up the passport forms to start the process. When we opened the door to enter, the security blocked me and told me I was not properly dressed to enter. I asked him what he meant.

His response was that I cannot enter the office wearing a sleeveless blouse and a pair of shorts with sandals. I stepped back and said, "What do you mean I am not properly dressed? I am wearing a pair of Bermuda shorts and a sleeveless blouse. What about this is improper?" He said it is the law and I cannot enter. I responded by saying I was only going in to get two copies of the passport forms.

He told me I have to stand outside, and he will get the forms for me. I waited outside and looked at my husband in total shock. We got the forms and went away.

Our next stop was to take the photographs for the passports. We noticed that a studio was a few doors from where we were. I said to my husband since we were parked already and there was a studio, let us have the pictures taken now and get it over with.

We went to the studio and asked if we could have our pictures taken for our passport now or if we have to make an appointment to come back. The clerk reply was we can have it done now, but I would have to cover up my sleeveless blouse because the passport office would not accept the pictures because of the way I am dressed.

I was also surprised of the comment. I told my husband to give me his shirt to put it over my blouse, and he can have his picture taken afterwards. I dressed in my husband's shirt, they took the pictures, and all our photographs are showing us in the same shirt.

Some of the churches will tell you that if you are to take part in a funeral you cannot have any parts of your bodies exposed.

The other extreme that I have noticed is that you cannot take a bottle of water with you to drink into some of these government offices. If you have the water bottle, you have to go outside to drink the water but not inside the office. How can such a law be enforced when Jamaica is such a hot climate?

The lines for most government offices in Jamaica are always very long; even if you are sitting, you have to wait a while. And with the process of going outside to drink the water, someone will take the seat you were sitting on when you come back inside.

Bag, Shoes, and Clothes

This is a good time to talk about the problem with clothes, bags, and shoes.

These items are certainly a problem for us. They do not last any time in Jamaica.

This is also an easy embarrassment; you are all dressed up and at a function, and by the time the function is over, the sole of your shoes are gone. The bags are stripping right in front of yours eyes.

I have now learned to travel with an extra pair of shoes. It does not matter if these items are leather. They will dry rotten. It does not matter how you try to store them; they still fall apart.

If you don't wear the clothes you have often, they will also cause a problem. They will change color on you especially the white clothes. These clothes even if you wash and iron or dry clean them, once you leave them for a while, they are still a problem.

My suggestion is that all these items that we spend so much money on, try and give them away. Don't bring them here because they will not be of any benefit.

The other suggestion is that if after reading this book and anyone has any idea on how to protect these items and make them last, please share the information. This returning resident is opened for suggestions on how to protect my clothes, bags, and shoes.

Towels and Sheets

The towels and sheets that are not used very often will give you a surprise when you are ready to use them. When you unfold them, you'll realize that you cannot use them. The white linens are the worst; they will turn yellow, or they have quite a lot of yellow spots all over. The answer to such problems is to use these things as often as possible. Don't let anything sit around and not be used. The other solution is not to have a lot of anything. The biggest problem I find is how quickly things dry rotten.

I was given a hint after talking to someone a few days ago, and she recommended that I used a humidifier in the room where I have the clothes. This I have not tried yet.

CHAPTER 15

Labour Laws in Jamaica for Housekeepers and Gardeners

One of the first things when you settle in your house is to think about a gardener and a helper. Most people are thinking should they hire a full-time helper or a part-time or a day worker.

If you are thinking of a full-time helper, my advice to you is to first go to the ministry of labour and meet with a counselor and talk. Get the information, make notes, and do not leave without the leaflet.

I am writing from experience. The helpers and gardeners know everything about the policy and laws of the ministry as if they are the ones who wrote the book.

They are not afraid to take you to the labour board; they are very knowledgeable, so therefore, you better know the labour laws yourself.

A few tips about full-time workers:

a. They are entitled to ten days sick leave with pay per year.

b. They are entitled to fourteen vacation days with pay.

c. They are entitled to all the holidays with pay.

d. If you ask them to work on any of those days, you have to pay them wages for time and a half.

e. If you have to let them go, you have to pay them all that they are entitled to receive.

A few tips about part-time workers:

a. It depends on how many hours it adds up to at the end of the week.

b. Over certain amount of hours, they are classified as full time.

c. If they are classified as full time, you have the responsibility of paying them and treating them as full-time workers with all the benefits.

This is why it is in your best interest to visit with the ministry of labour before you decide upon hiring any workers.

A few tips about day workers:

If a day worker is in the best interest for your purpose, then you have no contract binding with that worker. The only duty you have is you agree with the cost of the day's work. If it involves lunch, you are responsible to give them lunch. If the agreement does not involve lunch, you pay the amount and that is it for the day until next time.

There are some information the police asks you to have if you are to hire someone to work in your house:

1. Get the person who you hire to get a police record.

2. Have their full names and addresses.

3. Take a picture of the worker.

The police visited churches and community centres asking that you are to have all these information ready. Many times when there is a problem and the police will call you, the person has no information to present to the police.

The other good thing and a great idea is when the person you are hire has been recommended by someone you know.

The other hint about a worker, especially a gardener, is that they are very difficult. Even though you are the one paying them and you are the one who hired them, they don't want you to tell them how you want things to be done.

They easily have attitude. It doesn't matter how long they worked with you and if you believe that you have something very good going with them.

They fail to realize that it is your place and this is how you want it done. They will be the first to tell you that it is not going to look good. Often times your desires are being overlooked and an individual's perspective is being forced on you.

They are not paying attention to details in order to have an outcome reflective of your choices. After all, it is your decision. All they have to do is to just do what you asked them to do. It has nothing to do with them.

These are the problems I have with the workers. Even the contractor who is building your house is ready to change your blueprint to put it the way they think it should be.

And a last bit of advice about your workers, whether they are full time or part time: please keep a record of the weeks ending and have them sign for their pay.

CHAPTER 16

Maintenance of the House

The Sun and the Sea

There are a few things you would not believe would be a problem for the houses in Jamaica. These things also cause major maintenance problems to the house. They are also the most beautiful things in the country; it is the sun and the sea.

Reading this, you are wondering what I am talking about and how these could be problems.

When I was building my house, I used to love driving around the neighborhood to admire the other houses. I could not understand how come Jamaica is such a bright, radiant country but the houses did not have a lot of bright colors.

I would also go to the hardware stores to look at the colors in the stores thinking that they did not have bright colors. The stores do have bright and radiant colors, but there is a problem. I have noticed this house that was painted a beautiful papaya color. The color surely caught my eyes, and you can't help but notice this house.

I have noticed after about two years the color of the house started to fade away; finally, it was now a light pink. The sun burned the color.

The roof on our house was a radiant orange, but now the color has also faded. The warranty on the roof is twenty-five years, but as for the color, there is no warranty.

One of the things that I was looking forward to do when I lived in Jamaica was to have my clothes washed and put on the clothesline. I wanted to have the sun and the wind blowing my clothes; no more machines drying. I was looking forward to going back to nature.

The problems started a few months after hanging the clothes to dry; all the colors are no longer bright and vibrant. The hardest color I noticed was the color of navy blue. It was the easiest color to fade and to look terrible. The sun surely takes a toll on your clothes.

The sun will not just fade your clothes' color, but it will also be a problem for your furniture inside the house and the curtains.

When you have the windows closed and the blinds at the windows, you believe you are safe. The problem is that all is needed is the glare of the sun to come into the house. The glare of the sun will change the color of your furniture. The things you have in white will also change to a light yellow.

The furniture, whether they are inside the house or on the patio or whether they are exposed directly to the sun or the light, it does have an effect on them. The colors on the flowerpots on the patio, unless they are made of concrete, will fade.

The Sea Salt

The sea salt is a major problem for the burglar bars anywhere around the house, the rot iron around the fence, and the bars around the front porch. The sea salt is havoc for this kind of material. These bars needed constant painting and replacing because the sea salt eats away at the material and causes them to rot. The lamp shades will also crumble to dust from the sea spray.

Toilets

The toilets have two problems:

    a.   The pressure of the water

    b.   The lime in the water

The pressure of the water causes the toilet to constantly leak. When you flush the toilet, the pressure to fill the tank, even when it is turned down low, still causes the float not to settle. The toilets require lots of maintenance, and you have to always call the plumber for adjustments.

The tanks also have a problem because of the amount of lime in the water. When you look inside the tank, you can see how much the lime accumulated and cause hardness inside the tank.

The pressure of the water in the toilet tanks causes the toilets to have a little water slightly dripping down the side of the toilet and it will turn yellow and hard. There is nothing to clean the toilet if you see that little rust in the toilet. The only cleaning product that I can use to clean the toilet is a product with lime in the ingredients.

Unwelcome Animals and Insects

Unwelcomed animals and insects are the rats, the roaches, bullfrogs, mosquitoes, ants, and flies.

Remember that we are now living in the island, so we will have problems with these animals and insects like rats, roaches, bullfrogs, mosquitoes, ants, flies, and the lizards.

The first thing is that you can't be afraid of them and live in Jamaica. This kind of fear will only make your life miserable.

There is some maintenance to be done, and you have to get the insect control to do the land before the house is completed and the house before you even move into it and the yard also. After the first pest control is done, you have to have it done according to how you are having problems with the unwanted.

The Rats

The rats are the ones that you'll have no idea how they get into your house.

The only thing I can suggest is that all the doors that are exposed to the outside must have protection under the door that not even ants can crawl under. The other thing is to keep the door closed at all times.

As for the doors that are opened to the kitchen from outside, put French doors or sliding doors so that when you close them, you can have the light coming in, and you don't feel boxed in.

The other thing is to keep a rat trap handy; the best ones are the old-fashioned kind. Also, keep the ones with the paste for the mice along with the rat baits for outside around the yard. This you need to constantly throw around the yard.

The other problem is if there is a vacant lot beside you; the rats will live there in the bushes.

The Roaches

I don't know for anywhere else but the area where I am I can see the roaches flying. The problem for me could be because I have an empty lot beside me. I also noticed that they are more plentiful when it seems that it is going to rain. So the best thing to do is to make sure your doors and windows are closed if you do not have mesh at the windows.

I know some people who have problems with the teenager roaches. They bring in the companies to fumigate the yard and house but still have problem.

The Lizard, the Flies, and the Mosquitoes

The best protection for the lizard, the flies, and the mosquitoes is to have your windows with a mesh. The windows can be opened and you can have the nice breeze and don't have these insects living on the inside with you in the house.

The other thing is not to keep your property bushy around the house or to have areas where water can settle; otherwise, you will not be able to get rid of the mosquitoes.

The Frogs

The frogs I have no solutions for. They are out at night in full and will hide anywhere in the day when you can't see them. In the mornings you know that they were there because of the mess they leave behind around in the yard and on the steps.

CHAPTER 17

Volunteering and Giving Back

When you have made the decision to come back to Jamaica and you are settled in and you are now living here for good, I know that you are retired and are putting your feet up to relax.

I have to say to all who are here and who are coming in the near future, you all have the experience to make a difference, and we all have to do something.

We can't feel that because we have built the wall fence; the burglar bars are up, the steel gate is up, and we now have the gate opener. Nothing else is our concern; I don't have to care. I just have to go out, get what I want, and take the plane when I feel like.

We have made the decision to come home, so let us start caring and change our thinking. Whether you want to or not, you must get involved. Jamaica has a lot of work to be done. We can make a difference by starting to volunteer. We need to continue giving; we can't stop. There are numerous service clubs here in Jamaica and very reputable international organizations.

These organizations can be beneficial to each and every one of us. The more we organize, the more things we get done. We can change Jamaica for the better one child at a time or one project at a time.

Whether we are going to start with our church or community, we must start somewhere. My son who lives in the USA was visiting with his family one summer holiday. I was talking to him about the cost of books for the children to go back to school here in Jamaica. He turned to me and said, "Can you imagine if all the Jamaicans who have migrated overseas were to sponsor one child for school what a Jamaica this would be?"

To start sponsoring one child, we don't have to spend a lot of money. We can start with our house-keeper's or our gardener's child. We can start with the books. All you asked for from that child is a copy of their report card. If that child is progressing or improving, the next year you can go a little further. The books and the uniforms next; the other year you can go a little further. You are helping the child; you don't have to give the money to the parents.

The schools give the list of books that the children need for school; you take the list and pick up the books from the bookstores and send it home with their mother or father. My son has sponsored a child. He bought the books and sent the books home to the child. The cost of the books was ten thousand Jamaican dollars; that is the first start.

Most Jamaicans come back to Jamaica very often; some of us now move back. Let us start with one child. Let us start with the bus fare and the lunch money to get the child to school. Most parents cannot afford to send the child or children to school. We can start with three hundred Jamaican dollars per day; that is one child we are taking off the street and the gangs. It can take so little to make such a big difference and change Jamaica one child at a time.

We can start by asking your family and friends from Jamaica. They can start with the school they attended: the primary the high school, the college, or the university.

There are many students in Jamaica who are doing very well but can't afford to continue their studies because of financial difficulties.

If you would like to get involved, call the principal, e-mail the principal, and most teachers have computers today. The principal will know the child who needs help. The principal will know the child who has the potential but because of wants and needs is not able to attend school. The principal and the teachers together will help you help a child.

I learned through my journey, especially in Jamaica, that no matter what we should try our best to give back. I learned that opportunity is a great thing. Let us help give a child that opportunity. At least we tried.

Most of our grandchildren overseas are very fortunate; they are blessed. I am not saying that it is easy; we know that it is hard work. This is a great opportunity to introduce our grandchildren about the concept of giving back.

Show them how they can make a difference in a child's life by giving to that child; it can be a programme at the church you attended where some children need help.

Your grandchild can start by saving the money that they get for allowance or say, "I want to save to buy a book for this little girl who is my friend in Jamaica."

The families who live overseas and travel to Jamaica could start by adopting a school. Let's start with a library or let's get them new books. The schools in Jamaica need a lot of help, just ask the principals.

I talk about funerals in Jamaica in a chapter and the things that people do with their money for a funeral—the waste.

This is an example of a very special project that my family has done for the community. This is about our parents' memorial service and headstones. We are from a large family of eleven children, grandchildren, and great-grandchildren.

The church that we grew up attending in the district was the same church my parents were members of until my mother passed away at the age of eighty-six.

This little church is one hundred years old and is built on a hill. My family decided that instead of spending the money on the most expensive headstones for our parents, we will give back to the community.

I called the church steward and asked what the church would like to be done at this time. She told me that the church is in need of quite a few things. My husband, the steward, and I set a time when we could meet at the church. I wrote the list of things and told her that I was not making any promises because this is a family decision, and I will get in touch with her as soon as we make a decision.

The next week, we met with the mason and the carpenter in the district and asked them if they could meet with us at the church. They are not members of the church, but they respected my mother and father and will do anything to help. My husband and I went to the church; we met the men and told them about our plans to have some work done on the church.

They were ready to get involved and that their day's pay was a certain amount but will work for half the price of their day's pay.

We measured all that was needed to be done. My husband calculated the amount of material needed to complete the project. The next stop was to the hardware store where we asked for a price of all the materials and delivery. The owner of the store gave us a price and told us he would give us the material at cost price and would deliver the material free. He said he is doing his part, and if we can do this, he too can do something for the community.

We also needed a welder, so on our way home, we stopped to see a welder and told him the measurements that have to be welded and his cost.

He wasn't even from the district, but when we told him that we were doing this for the community, he volunteered his time.

I have all the information to present to the family meeting when we gathered to plan for the memorial for our parents. The meeting took place, and we all agreed that instead of spending the money on buying the most expensive headstones we would buy two beautiful headstones and give back to the church and the community.

The family meeting even got more exciting because we were all feeling good about our decision to give back. During the meeting, I told my siblings that I was thinking of us doing something more for the church and the community. I told them that I was thinking that we should not just have the memorial services for our parents but for us to go back twenty-five years in the church and have a memorial service for the other members who have passed and was never remembered.

Our family meeting ended on a high note, and we were ready to get things started.

We notified the church steward that our family will be doing all the work on what they have requested.

We told the church steward about our plans to have the memorial service including the members of the church, and we are asking for the list of names going back to twenty-five years. We also asked her if she could get in touch with the members of the deceased members and invite them for the memorial service. I notified her of the days we will be working at the church so she could have all the members to be part of that day along with the community.

The day of the work, this is how the morning started: There was a young lady about twenty-one years old who asked us all to hold hands, and she prayed. In her prayers, she gave thanks that God had answered her prayers. She had prayed for this day for such a long time, and it finally came to past. Prayers are answered if you keep the faith.

After the prayer, there was not a dry eye in that church; everyone was happy. The thing that really touched me also was the children and the young adults; they would go up on the ladder cleaning with the broom, the mop, the cloth, and the dusters. My family provided the lunch, and my brother cooked for us that day.

When the work was completed, this is what my family has done for the church and the community: We have welded one hundred and fifty feet of galvanized steel. The members finally have something to hold on to while climbing the stairs. The church needed repairs, and we tiled the areas of the church that needed to be completed. We painted a section of the church. We cleaned the church from ceiling to the floor, and we had the church sign redone.

There are some amazing things that can come together just by giving back:

a. My family got all the grandchildren involved. They were part of the planning. They were the ones who were financially responsible for the repairs of the church.

b. We got the community involved even if they did not attend that church.

c. The business people got involved, and they gave something back.

d. We had a community get-together in fellowship, eating and drinking, while we worked together.

The day of the memorial we had people from all over Jamaica, even from overseas, attend the memorial service. It was an amazing service as each and every name was called; there was a pause just for you to reflect. One person told me after the service that as each name was called, the memories brought them back as a young man growing up seventy years ago.

There was about five hundred people who attended that memorial service.

The other thing that was touching at this memorial was that we saw other people that we had not seen since we left school. Some of us thirty years, some forty years, and some fifty years; this was not just a memorial service, but it was a family reunion of the community, our schoolmates, and our church.

After the church service, my family invited the congregation to join us for brunch at our family house a little distance from the church.

The day before the memorial service, my family had our parents' headstones placed on the graves. We all had quite day as the family was eating, drinking, laughing, and talking about our memories of our parents.

In my own words, to complete that weekend, it was a reunion in the flesh and in the memories of all the deceased loved ones. I am hoping that after reading this book that some of the readers will be inspired to make a difference; it doesn't matter how simple.

CHAPTER 18

Funerals

I am amazed at how funerals in Jamaica are such a big event. Rich and poor and in between, most Jamaicans will spend their last dollar for a big event for a funeral. It seems to me that funerals are the place to get dressed up and have a good time; there are lots of food and music. This is the place to socialize and in Jamaican funerals is a large crowd.

I do not have a problem with you wanting to bury your loved ones with respect and dignity. The things I noticed when it comes to burying your dead is that the last right for that person is a big event. I noticed that it does not matter how that person was living as long as there is a big finally to end that journey; that is all that matters.

Through my journey since I am back living in Jamaica, I have overheard conversations of people talking about how grand they would like their funeral to be. They are making sure they have cows and goats to sell.

These people that are talking about the goat or the cow at the bush are not saying that is to take them to the doctor when they are sick. Or I don't care how much the medication cost; I will buy it to get better. The most important thing is that when they are dead, there must be money to have the big celebration.

The other thing I noticed is that some of these people have relatives who live overseas. The effort is not about looking after them while they are alive, but as soon as they passed, they pay a plane fare, stay in a hotel, then they go to the funeral home, pay this exorbitant amount of money to buy the expensive package that included the band and all the other things that go with it including the expensive casket.

I have witnessed with my own eyes here in Jamaica of some unbearable condition of family members—the condition of how they live. I was told by a very close friend of my mine that on one occasion she came to bury her mother. She went next door after the funeral to visit the neighbour to say hello to her because she is not able to move around.

My friend was in a state of shock because this old lady was not well cared for. The lady told her how difficult it was for her and she was not happy and wished she was the one that had passed on.

There are children who come from overseas to see their loved ones but can't stay where they are staying. They stay somewhere else, and they take taxi and visit.

This means that if they are there for one week or so, they travel by taxi every day to come and visit. They will not stay at the house where their loved one is living because it is not convenient for them to stay. This location does not have a shower, running water, or an indoor toilet.

I have known of people who died of hunger but the children then give them a big farewell.

What is it about this big funeral in Jamaica? Although we are not in a position to have a big funeral, our loved ones are so determined to have one. They will do anything to have this massive celebration. I have

Coming Home

so many experiences about funerals here in Jamaica. The problem I find is that as long as the person knows you or because maybe you went to school with them or from the neighbourhood as a child, they are asking you to help to bury someone from the area.

They are begging you to help, but they are wearing a large button with the person's face on it. I had to ask one person who is asking me if I can help with the funeral expensive how he got the button and how much it cost to print it.

This big money spending on funerals in Jamaican, why is it so? Who are they doing it for? The dead or for themselves? Let us stop and take a good look at what we are doing.

Again, I am not saying not to bury your loved one with dignity, but if we do what we have to do for that loved one when they are alive, then there is no reason to give away the money for an expensive funeral. What is this about a glass casket, the marching band, the horse-drawn casket, and the Hummer carrying the casket? Did this person ever have a Hummer when they were alive?

Just imagine if you make a conscious decision to even spend 50 percent of what you spend to bury your loved one and keep back that money to help yourself or the children of that loved one who is deceased?

I have witnessed so many sad stores in regard to families burying their loved ones. The things they do to have a big splash to impress people that they have money; they will use their children's education funds to

193

have the biggest funeral even with the limousine because there is no insurance for the funeral or inheritance.

Let's start thinking smart. When we spend the money to have this big celebration, who are we giving the money to? How much debt do we owe after this big event?

Have you ever stopped to think about the funeral homes that you pay all this pile of money to for this festivity? These businesses are a bottomless pit; you have to pay that money before the body can leave that funeral home. They are collecting the money from you Jamaicans for a mitt or for a feel-good time. You don't have to spend all that money.

That loved one is at peace; they are not asking for you to do any of this. Jamaicans, stop spending your hard-earned money foolishly. Do the right thing for yourself; do the right thing while that person is still alive.

Writing this chapter in this book is for a reason. The reason is that I hope the returning residents are making a difference in Jamaica in getting things done by coming together. They are also going to make a difference in this area that they are not going to get caught up with this big money spending on funerals.

There is so much we can do in the memory of a loved one who had passed. Instead of spending the money for this big funeral, let us start thinking about the schools, the hospitals, the church, a child in the community, a family in the community that needs help, or sponsoring a child. There are many more ideas under the chapter of volunteering and giving back.

CHAPTER 19

Tips for Moving into Your House

a.   You must fence your yard.

b.   You must have a gate.

c.   You must put security on your house.

d.   You must have mesh on your windows.

e.   Pay attention to your neighbourhood.

f.   If you are not expecting anyone, don't be too quick to open your gate or door.

g.   Stay away from intercom at your gate. If you expect someone, they will call you in advance.

h.   You must have water backup.

i.   You must have your property well lit.

j.   You must have a booster for your vehicle.

k.   You must have a charger for your tire.

l.   You must have the electricity grounded.

m. You must have a lightning rod.

n.   Know where the hospital, public or private, is located.

o.   Know someone you can call.

p.   Have the number of a taxi.

q.   Know where the post office is.

r.   Know where the police station is.

s.   Have the telephone number for the police station.

t.   Before you hire a gardener or a house keeper, it is best to go to the ministry of labor office.

u.   Keep a copy of the labour law.

v.   For the person you have hired for work, it is best to have someone recommend them to you.

w.   Have full names and address of workers.

x.   Have a plumber's telephone number you can call and trust to fix a problem.

y.   Have an electrician's telephone number just in case.

z.   Watch the bags that are coming in your gate so you know what is going out.

aa. The last best thing to be home is when someone is working inside your house.

Differently

I have lived overseas for thirty-seven years and returned to Jamaica. I lived here for six years before I started writing this book. My husband lived overseas for over sixty years. After living here, I started to wonder if this is home.

It could never be home; I did not feel at home. I started to question myself about the decision of coming home. How could it be home when I am feeling so apart from everything? My friends are not here; everything is different.

The Jamaica we know does not exist anymore. This is a different country. This is a simple example: remember the grand market (Christmas Eve) that we love to spend all evening going to and having fun? We would not dare ourselves to go out there in this kind of atmosphere because we are afraid, and we are not strong anymore.

We have also grown away from that kind of lifestyle. But this is the Jamaica that we know and dream of.

We come home because of the warm climate in Jamaica; the winter is very harsh on most of us, so we feel the best place is to come home. We build beautiful houses with the intention of enjoying it to the fullest.

We wish for the grandchildren and friends and other family members to come and enjoy the beautiful time with us.

We burglar bar around the house and all the windows and even the porch the gate is also fit with the remote button.

We make sure that we have everything to make us comfortable. This is my question: how many of us see the moon shine by sitting on our front porch at night?

Although we are here living in Jamaica. Are we enjoying Jamaica to its fullest? We get away from the cold, and our dream is to enjoy the beautiful weather in Jamaica. How many of us enjoy the cool breeze by sitting on our front porch in the evening? How many of us are sitting on our front porch talking to our neighbour?

We are now living just like when we were aboard; the question for us coming home is this: what is the difference between living overseas and living in Jamaica?

The answer is the beautiful weather; we are not cold and do not have to battle the snow.

This is our new trend that we have now started with our new friends; if we are lucky to have other returning residents as friends, we gather each other and we book into the hotel from Christmas Eve until Boxing Day.

We are now creating our Christmas with our new friends, not with the local friends or family if you have any living here. So you too have changed. These are the things we must and should take into consideration before we take this very important new start.

The question then is, how then can we say we are coming home? See, we are not friends with any of the locals. We have nothing in common. Even if we go to church, we are sticking with returning residents if any attend that church.

If and when we attend church and as soon as church is over, we are gone, or we even leave before the service is over because we do not want to mix.

The other problem with us returning residents is that we are like a sore thumb. We are always sticking out.

How then we say we come home when we can't even been treated fairly in the market? The prices changes as soon as they see you coming. If you think you can pretend not to be noticed, don't waste your time; they know who you are.

The other problem is we have a helper who is in our house, but unfortunately, we can't trust them. They do not respect you because there is a resentment if you are a returning resident.

After a few months, some of us are very lucky if they stay with us. We let them go because we no longer feel like they are working to the quality of what you expected or they decide to quit. You are in for a rude awaking for when after they are gone, you have noticed so much is missing.

I am not saying that all helpers are all the same; there are some terrific hardworking and honest ladies who work for you, and they will protect and care for you and respect their job. I am not saying not to come home, but most people I spoke to have had enough and returned to their country of citizenship. They all say if they know what they know now, they would have done it differently.

Returning Residents

I have noticed that some returning residents when they buy land they buy land with precipice. We have to remember that when most of us are coming home, we are already in our sixties and over. The land should be level so we can get our exercise walking around the yard picking the fruits that we planted.

We have to think about our health that we can't walk around the yard that is not level because most of us have the famous arthritis and lots of pain.

We also have to take into consideration the house that we plan to build. Why are we building these houses with so many different levels?

How are we going to go up and down the stairs? We have to start thinking when we are building our house to build a bungalow.

If we feel that we need something a bit higher, do not build higher than two floors. If it is a two-story, please put a bedroom on the main floor; you would be glad you did.

This is an advice you will be glad you take seriously; it is about your bathrooms. We have to think about our bathrooms just like how we think of our stairs and yard that is not level.

The shower in your bathrooms is very dangerous when you have a bath. When you are in Jamaica, you don't take a lot of baths. If the time is hot, you take a quick shower instead of a bath. This is my advice: make a separate shower, and if you need a bath, make it separate but do not have a shower in the bath.

It is an accident waiting to happen; when you use the soap, the bath is very slippery, and when you are of a certain age, you do not have that support to handle that bath.

The best thing to do for your shower is to have no bath but have a built-in seat. Have a handheld showerhead; you will be glad you did that because you can be independent for a long time without having anyone to help you in the shower. If you make these preparations from the beginning, you will not need a chair to sit in the shower. They sure will come in handy for that day, and you will not lose your independence.

Here are a few tips that I know will be of great benefit to you; some of these tips you are not even aware of.

a. In the banks when you go to get money, don't stand at the counter and count your money after the teller hands it to you. Pay attention while the cashier is counting.

b. If you have to take a large sum of cash, ask the teller to let you pick it up inside and out of sight of everyone. The bank will accommodate you.

c. When you go into your vehicle, please lock your doors.

d. Women, please do not leave your bags open on the backseat with the windows down.

e. If you do not know the person, don't give the person a ride.

f. When you are out in the public, be aware at all times.

g. If you have to have a bite while you are out shopping, look at your surroundings and be careful of your conversation. You don't know who is listening.

h. In the public, especially at the market places, you can easily be distracted. Be careful with your money.

i. Don't take all your money into the market or public places.

j. Men, don't take out a bundle of money from your pocket all at once, either have it in a small amount or in your wallet.

k. Only take the money with a few extra dollars you will be spending that day.

Returning Residents
Can Be Their Worst Enemies

This is a conversation I overheard in a restaurant one day:

There were three people sitting at a table behind me, and they were talking about the experience that they had with customs and clearing the container.

I listened to this conversation and could tell how many flat screen big televisions was in that container, how many stoves, washing machines, how many new and how many old appliances were in that container, and how much money was paid to customs. I also know that the stove was electric.

I know where this man will be going for his next holiday and when he is planning to go. All this conversation took place in a burger joint; this could be anybody sitting there listening to the conversations. I want you to image what could happen when these people leave to go home. I know their names; I know so much about them. The next journey for these people is that they are not aware that they are been followed.

Returning resident, remember you have got to be more careful. Jamaica is not the Jamaica you know; it has changed.

Returning Residents Association

This organisation is very popular amongst the returning residents; there is a chapter in all the parishes. Some parishes have more than one. The Returning Residents Association is a network of returning residents who get together to support one another to keep their memories alive.

They also need each other to comfort one another when things go wrong and when no one else will listen and would understand their feelings.

These groups are also active in the communities. These returning residents all have their stories; some are happy and some are sad. Within the organization, they also do their part to help a child and other things. They will work together to help the community that they are living in to work for better road or water. Some returning residents will spend their money to fix some things in the communities.

This community is a very good source to contact for information about the community you are planning to live in. Most returning residents are also living in gated communities and will tell you about that community. Returning residents are very active especially in the gated communities.

Neighbourhood watch is another resource to get information about the community. There are many active neighbourhood watch; they have signs around the area. Talk to someone from the neighbourhood, and they will tell you about the meetings.

Returning Residents and Opportunities

Jamaica has lots of opportunity for educated and business opportunities. What is needed are some young entrepreneurs to come home and get our young people working. If you are smart and talented, come and take a look at what you can do for Jamaica.

Coming Home Finally

You build your dream home; the trailer arrives and you clear customs with all the stress and frustration gone. It takes you weeks to unpack the container and put everything in its place.

You are now ready to put your feet up and ready to enjoy home. No worries, you are home.

A few months after living in your house, the nightmare started. A heavy shower of rain started to fall; you have never seen so much rain. You notice the chair in the bedroom is soaking wet, and you realize that the roof is leaking.

The next thing you notice is the water running under the windows and the brand-new toilets are leaking. The hot water is not coming into some of the showers. There is no light in the pool; the only way to fix the pool is drain the water.

The wall around the house is breaking away, and you have to rebuild.

The electrician was hired by the contractor; you now have many electrical problems. Just to be told by someone that the electrician was not a licensed electrician.

The plumber—although you pay so much money to install all the toilets and showers—has no idea how to install them, and he has never seen these before. They are all leaking.

The contractor for the kitchen still believe that you owe him money although you paid in full.

The problem I believe is that these contractors do not have any idea how to make an estimate.

The other problem is that after a few years living in the house you are now faced with almost redoing everything all over.

You believe that you have enough money to come home and be comfortable. All the things you did not anticipated you are faced with so many things to be done. You have not included maintaining the house because you practically rebuilt the house.

This last question I will let you answer after all this…

How much money do you have left?

This book will make a difference and will surely guide you so that you will not have to answer the question above because it would never happen to you.

It is very hard to start over from the beginning after you retire.

If I Knew What I Know Now

This is how I would have done it:

a. I would not invest that much money in Jamaica.

b. I would build a smaller house.

c. I would have a condo in my country of citizenship.

d. I would spend only a few months in Jamaica each year.

e. I would not come home to Jamaica for good.

Home

a. Where is home?

b. Home is where the heart is.

c. Home is where you lived longer than where you were born.

d. Home is where you built friendship.

e. Home is where you raised your children.

f. Home is where you built relationships.

g. Home is where you feel comfortable.

h. Home is where you are accepted.

i. Home is where you have no fear,

j. Home is where no one is out to get you.

k. Home is where you live in peace.

l. Home is where the people around don't believe you owe them.

m. Home is where you are free.

n. Home is where you are happy.

o. Home is where you watch the grandchildren have fun and see them as often as possible.

p. Home is where lots of laughter and noise are.

q. Home is where you can open your door any time of the day without fear.

r. Home is where you walk around the neighbour-hood without fear.

s. Home is where you sit on your patio without fear.

t. Home is where you open your windows and let in the cool breeze flow.

Jamaica Land We Love

The coming home we have dreamed and worked so hard to achieve is bittersweet. Jamaica is not the Jamaica we know; the people have changed. Jamaica the country has changed just like how we, the returning residents, have changed. There are many returning residents who have walked away from everything in Jamaica. The dream and hope is that one day there will be a buyer for the house. Some have gone back home because of the crime and the robbery. Some have gone back because they are a target. Some have gone back because of the attack on them. Some have gone back because they can't find peace and happiness as they have hope and wish for. Some returning residents have returned because, unfortunately, they just can't live here again due to too many problems. Some have returned because of the cost of health care in Jamaica is too expensive. When I talk to those who are going back to their country of citizenship, and I told them about this book and why I am writing, they all say one thing: they wish they had a book like this to read because they would have done things differently.

So many returning residents are not coming back because of the theft of their money, and they are not able to complete their houses; when they think the house is finished, they have no money and no house.

There are so many unfinished houses all over Jamaica because during the process of building so many things have gone wrong. They will not continue building, and they are not selling it either. Their hope is that things will be different one day. They have not given up hope for Jamaica; they are still praying for peace. They are hopeful that Jamaica will be one day the land of paradise and that their children or grandchildren will benefit. They also know they will not live to see this happen and will not live to reap it. All the returning residents have a story whether they are here or they have returned.

A lot of returning residents are also happy to be here and consider it as their home. Maybe they have done it right. This book is our story—Roy and Blondel Reid. My hope is that after reading this book you will learn through our journey and make the right decision.

This book is not only for Jamaicans, but for all the other countries, especially the Caribbean Islands. The concept of this book is to take these questions and use them where they can be beneficiary to you.

There is so much information in this book that will help you to make the right decision.

Regrets

I wish I knew what I know now; and I wish I had this book. I would have done things differently. But we are here, and we are making the best of it. Wish you all good luck.

God bless you all.

Bureau of Standards : www.bsj.org.jm

National Water Commission : www.nwcjamaica.com

Jamaica Public Service: www.myjpsco.com

Customs: www.jacustoms.gov.jm

Fire Arm Licensing Authority: www.fla.gov.jm

National Solid Waste Management Authority:
http://www.nswma.gov.jm/

Registrars General Department: http://www.rgd.gov.jm/

The Consolate's Office, Passport, Immigration
and Citizenship Agency: www.pica.gov.jm

National Land Agency of Jamaica: http://www.nla.gov.jm/

Tax Registration No., Property Tax, Drivers License:
http://www.jamaicatax.gov.jm/

Returning Resident Association: http://www.jis.gov.jm/